LUCKY PARCHMENT

NO. CONTAINING

The Great Humanist

GURU NANAK

by

SIR JOGEDNRA SINGH

&

RAJA SIR DALJIT SINGH

Nirmal Publishers & Distributors

B-2, Vishal Enclave New Delh!-110027

Published by :
NIRMAL PUBLISHERS & DISTRIBUTORS
B-2, Vishal Enclave, New Delhi-110027
Phone ; 5413460

Reprint – 1987

Price : Rs 200-00

Printed at :
ANUBHAV ART PRESS, 9-DSIDC, RAGHUBIR NAGAR, NEW DELHI-27

FOREWORD

Prophets appearing at different times and periods have spoken of the truth which it was their mission to bring to humanity to cure the sickness of the soul. They give it in words and forms suited to the needs of times, climes and people, and just as the colour of cows vary, but the colour of the milk is white, so the truth revealed by prophets remains unchanged and unchangeable.

The Guru came to show the true way, out of the darkness of superstition and formalism. He came to show the path of integration. He said that the law of life was to love one another and in that loving to awaken the spirit of devotion and find God.

He came to lift the humble and the down-trodden and to endow the weak and faltering with the power of faith. He came to save the people, broken up by castes and creeds and to teach them that they were children of one God.

The Guru in clear lucid language, showed us how to exercise free will and break off the fetters of our own forging. Salvation cannot be obtained, he said, by abandoning home or family or by wandering aimlessly, by torturing the body or frequenting holy places, by performances of external austerities, ceremonials or pouring oblation into sacrificial fires. It is by kindling the fire of devotion in the self itself and feeding it by the daily performance of duties, allotted under the divine command, that the sense of self is lost and the path of discipleship followed.

The Guru declared that he was neither a Hindu nor a Mussalman. He belonged to all and enjoined on all to worship the one God.

The word of the true teacher touched the hearts of all men, Hindus and Muslims, yogis and householders alike. The Guru drew their minds to one God by the power of the sacred name :

When the mind is tranquil
Like the limpid lake
And the path is made smooth
The light of the name enters the heart.
Hold fast in the heart the true name
It guides even the unseeing and the blind.

Guru Nanak has given the world a simple doctrine, a pure faith, universal in its application. Those who are eager to hear the Guru speak can resort to the sacred volume, Guru Granth Sahib. All those who are weary of the materialism of the modern times will find in the gospel of the Guru comfort, and the way of happy, healthful living on earth and beyond earth. The way is revealed in the clearest possible light ; follow it and discover the art of righteous living.

I must not anticipate what the reader must find for himself. Raja Sir Daljit Singh has gathered these treasures as offerings at the feet of the Guru. He caught a glimpse of Guru Nanak in his boyhood. He inherited from his great ancestor, Baba Jassa Singh, the seed of wisdom. His father fostered it and through his varied experiences in other lands and study of sacred books of all religions, he now in late years finds himself fit to undertake the great work of bringing the teachings of the Guru within the reach of all who do not know Gurmukhi. The gospel of Guru is given in the *shabads* of the Guru, and in the teachings which he gave through his long journey from one end of India to the other, Persia and Arabia.

The *shabads* have been so rendered that their meaning may become clear to those unfamiliar with our modes of thought and expression. If I have missed giving a literal rendering the fault is mine. The renderings are, however, subject to the original text of the *shabads* which is available for verification.

Aira Holme, Simla — JOGENDRA SINGH.

GURU NANAK

1469—1538 A. D.

Life—Travels—Teachings

CONTENTS

1. The age is like a drawn sword
2. Out of the cotton of compassion
3. "By sympathy and understanding," said the Guru
4. This body is the field
5. "What is that sickness ?" asked Hari Das
6. How has the money been wasted ?
7. "Regular work will draw him," argued Bibi Nanki
8. And his wife gave birth to two sons
9. "What does it matter if I become a king ?"
10. "My dear sister, humanity is my family"
11. "If I live millions of years on air alone"
12. "I have no caste," said the Guru
13. To the town of Sialkot
14. Sajjan fell at the Guru's feet
15. Death is nothing but a gateway to birth
16. Forgiveness is my mother
17. We shall call the village Kartarpur
18. Lahore seethes with poisonous oppression
19. With Sheikh Behram
20. "We belong to the One"
21. The Great Ones of the world are like an elephant
22. What is love?
23. "The path is dark and dreary," said the Sikh
24. The Kaaba : the house of God is everywhere
25. To lose the self is to become light
26. And a soundless sound will fill your heart
27. This jiva is like a fish
28. Plough your land with right action
29. Words to Babar
30. No power higher than truth
31. Message to Machander Nath
32. To seek within, not outside
33. "Your words are like shafts of light," said the Lama
34. In the land of Perpetual Snows
35. He meets Guru Gorakh Nath

36. "Learn to die to the world while living"
37. Listen, O people, and search your hearts
38. At Panipat, the abode of Shah Sharaf..
39. Fools wrangle about eating meat
40. At last the Guru reached Hardwar
41. Righteous living lights up the path of life
42. To Benares, the abode of Shiva
43. With the oars of faith
44. Through the forests of Assam
45. Kauda, the man-eating Bheel
46. Kamroop, seat of black magicians
47. Jagannath Temple and the music of his voice
48. The Six Schools of Philosophy and the Guru
49. "Come and be my disciple," said the Mahant
50. In Sangla Deep lived Raja Shiva Nabh
51. "In fear fire performeth its forced labour"
52. "What is Maya ?" asked the Rani
53. In the temple of Sri Rangam
54. On the banks of Narbada
55. "This house is impure," said the Brahman
56. "Elephant, rise"
57. To the birthplace of Krishna
58. "What is the right thing ?" asked the Guru
59. On the wheel of good action mould the container..
60. The earth is my Dharamsala
61. Tell me the difference between a Hindu and a Muslim
62. "What is the origin of sin ?" asked the Sikh
63. "What is it that lives and never dies ?"
64. Living the life of a householder
65. One day a Pandit came
66. What is the cause of pleasure and pain ?
67. At Kartarpur disciples gathered round the Guru
68. A party of Sadhus came
69. He who is conceited
70. My boat is now loaded
71. The Guru returned to Kartarpur
72. There lived in Village Khadur, Lehna
73. One day the disciples of Sheikh Behram
74. As pure as the water of the Ganges
75. When I am aware of my own self
76. On the banks of the river Ravi
77. Dispute arose among the Hindus and the Muslims

THIS WORLD OF OURS IS SUBJECT TO SUNSHINE & SHADOWS. The shadow-chaser is the shadow-maker also. Man inherits both the light of love and the gloom of hate. The Jiva, the soul, a spark from divine, descends to earth clothed in the darkness of the self and struggles for salvation.

Every individual inherits a *dharma*, his own conscience the light that never fails in revealing that love is the law of life and to transgress this law is to sin and to suffer.

All religions teach us that we are limbs of the same body and that truest worship is to serve our fellowmen ; to be helpful is to be happy. But men have war in their hearts, they delight in discord and perpetrate atrocious persecutions in the name of God, who is the Father of all. They give their lives in the name of religion and refuse to live it.

In any age or country in which godliness and selfless tendencies suffer an eclipse. Soverign Power passes into the hands of men, who cheated by desire to enslave others and exalt themselves, range nations against nations to pillage and to plunder. They make lawlessness not only permissible but praisworthy and cause moral and material devastation and ruin.

The Divine Law never fails or falters, as day follows night so good follows evil, peace persues war, righteousness overtakes unrighteousness. The storm of self is allowed to work itself out and God sends a true teacher to lead mankind from darkness to light. With the coming of a true teacher, the darkness of desire suffers a defeat and the sunshine of truth prevails. It is this truth which Shri Krishna in Bhagwad Gita declared

> "Whenever there is decay of righteousness and exaltation of unrighteousness then I myself come forth for the protection of the good. For the destruction of evil-doers and for the sake of firmly establishing righteousness I am born from age to age."

The true teacher holds aloft the torch of truth which destroys shadows and superstitions. He himself being the incarnation of love defeats the spirit of hate and distrust and leads misguided men to paths of goodness by the divinity of his own personality. He kindles into a flame of love the divine spark in every human heart.

India, in the fifteenth century and the centuries that preceded it, had experienced the march of invading armies, ruthless beyond description, massacring men without mercy in the name of religion and plundering hearths and homes without distinction. The people of India had forsaken their spiritual heritage and lost the art of united action and with it the power to defend themselves. In spite of their heroic traditions, without the firmness of faith in one God, they wasted their stock of noble emotions in the observance of endless ritual and taboos which robbed them of the power to unite and sapped the source of their strength. They were divided into castes and classes and small independent states at war with each other, in no position to snatch the sceptre from successive tyrants, who compelled them to accept subjection and serfdom. Guru Nanak himself said

The age is like a drawn sword,
The kings are butchers
In the gloom of falsehood
The moon of truth is never seen
And the law of life has taken wings.

In spite of the clear teaching of Bhagwad Gita that men should find in action the way of salvation, men lost in the maze of metaphysics ignored the truth that desireless action was essential to attain mental purification and with out proper purification the path of light was beyond reach.

The earth was weary of false doctrines, heresies and schisms, the unruly wills of men and their deceits and tyrannies, and was waiting for the appearance of a redeemer. Nature itself as if spell-bound swooned to welcome his advent. Peace reigned on earth that night. Yes, night indeed it was. but darkness was dispelled by the divine light of truth, which lit the heavens and all the earth beneath when he appeared all evil passions, anger, lust and desire retreated, while feelings of friendliness forbearance and forgiveness awakened in the desire-imbued hearts of men. Heavens and earth and the under-worlds echoed with the inaudible sound of the sacred name. In this auspicious moment, Sri Guru Nanak Dev came to earth. He came as prophets have always come—in a humble home and in a small village named Rai Bhoeki Talwandi, Punjab away from any seats of learning and culture. Blessed were they in whose midst he came and blessed were they who followed his light and live in his light now.

Guru Sahib's father, Mehta Kalu, was a Patwari—a rank which was fairly high in the Revenue Department in old times, his mother's name was Matta Tripat, and he had an elder sister named Bibi Nanki.

Mehta Kalu was also a landowner and was rich in a large herd of cattle. Rai Bular, the landlord held him in high esteem. He named his son after his daughter. His parents cherished the baby as the delight of their eyes. His mother nursed him with a loving care and discovered that he was unlike other babies. He never cried or clamoured for his mother as other babies did. He lay calmly in his cradle gazing upward with his deep luminous eyes. In due course he learned to walk and to speak, but he never played like other children of his age. He would sit as if lost in contemplation. He would give to other children his toys and persuade his mother to feed them on milk and buttered bread, wanting nothing for himself. The Guru was in his ninth year when his father on an auspicious day selected by his *prohit* (village priest) took his son to the village Pandit who ran a small school. He offered the Pandit a trayful of sweets and five rupees and prayed that he would accept Nanak as his pupil.

The Pandit received the child with pleasure, wrote out a few letters on a slate and asked the boy to repeat each letter after him. The Guru learned the alphabet in no time as though he had known it already. Then he turned to his teacher and asked.

" What are these letters meant for ? "

" Two or three letters make a word, words make sentences," repeated the Pandit, " and thus transmit knowledge and wisdom from age to age."

The Guru took the slate and sat aside lost in thought, joined the letters and formed words. The teacher turned to the Guru and saw he was sitting quietly, motionless, with his eyes fixed on the slate as though he was wholly absorbed in its contemplation.

" Why are you sitting as if struck dumb ? " asked the Pandit with impatience.

" I have joined the letters and formed a word," replied the Guru.

" What is it ? " asked the Pandit.

" I have made 'Soi'—Him," repeated the Guru.

" My son, what meaning are you trying to read in these simple symbols ? " asked the Pandit on receiving this unexpected reply.

" He who has created this Universe," said the Guru. " He is the One, He is the Lord of all."

" What more is passing through your little mind ? " asked the Pandit with an indulgent smile.

" Thus," said the Guru with conviction, " all learning is in vain, except to know Him and to serve Him."

The Pandit was astonished at the boy's precocity. " What do you know about Him ? " he asked.

" This, that to love Him is the end of knowledge and to forget Him is to forget the truth, even though one may carry a cartload of books," said the Guru.

The boy seemed to have passed into a state of ecstasy and spoke as if from some far away height. The Pandit was bewildered but wanted to test him and said, " God, of whom you speak, what is He and where is He ? "

" This creation is His," said the Guru, " and He is everywhere."

" Why cannot we feel Him and why cannot we see Him ? " asked the Pandit.

A flickering smile passed over the lips of the Guru as he answered : " Do the blind see the sun ? "

" No," said the Pandit.

" Are we not blind ? " asked the Guru. " Blind to all else, but sense-objects. He is beyond all senses and it is only when the darkness of the senses is removed that He can be seen. His love pervades all things."

" If His love is in all things, why are there chains and pains and sorrow and suffering ? " asked the Pandit.

" The answer is simple and you could have found it if you had searched your heart. When we act against the law of love, we forge fetters for ourselves, and entwine ourselves in the wheel of cause and effect," said the Guru.

" You mean we create Karma ? " asked the Pandit.

" Yes," said the Guru.

" It has been said by wise ones that with the fire of knowledge the seed of Karma can be permanently destroyed," remarked the Pandit.

" Yes, with realisation but not with book knowledge", said the Guru. " He alone is learned who knows Him."

The Guru then took up each letter of the alphabet and said, "As letters are symbols of speech, so myriads of forms are manifestations of God. He is the Enjoyer of all sense-objects. He is within and without all beings. He who knows that God is all and in all and consequently loses all sense of otherness, he alone escapes from the prison-house of "I-am-ness." In selfhood is bondage ; in losing the self, freedom."

The Pandit was not only astonished, but convinced that Nanak was an incarnation of God. He humbly bowed before his boy-pupil and took him to his father.

Mehta Kalu was sitting with some friends. He was surprised to see his son and his teacher coming back to him so early. Nanak must have played the truant and the Pandit must have brought him back to be reprimanded, he thought.

" Mehtaji, this son of yours is an Avatara, an incarnation of God and no ordinary mortal," said the Pandit as he took his seat near Mehta Kalu. " He has come to redeem the victims of Kalyug."

Mehta Kalu smiled incredulously. He was a worldly man and thought the Pandit was just flattering the boy. He wanted his son to be wise in the ways of the world, to know how to gain riches and power. So he said, " You are paying the boy a great compliment but I trust you will continue to instruct him."

" Instruct him ! How ? " exclaimed the Pandit. " He knows all that there is to be known."

" What does he know ? " asked Mehta Kalu.

" He knows more than I do," answered the Pandit. He knows :

1. God is One, Infinite without a second. He is the Author of all Creation.
2. He knows that to transgress the law of love is to sin.
3. He knows that ' I-am-ness ' is the disease and carries its own cure.

Tell me what more there is to know ? " said the Pandit.

Mehta Kalu looked at the Pandit with unbelieving eyes, but the Pandit rose and prostrated himself at the feet of the Guru and before departing again repeated : " Mehtaji, I am not a fool. I believe in what I have said, your son has all the characteristics of an Avatara."

2

YEARS SPED THEIR WAY, THE GURU REACHED THE AGE when he must be, according to the custom of his family, invested with the sacred thread.

Mehta Kalu made great preparations for the performance of the ceremony. He made elaborate arrangements for the entertainment of his guests—relatives, friends and others whom he invited. There was a great gathering on the appointed day at his house. Hardyal, the family *prohit*, was in great form. He had the courtyard floor replastered. On a raised platform he spread a woollen carpet and drew a circle round it, and then took his seat with all the accessories of the ceremony ranged round him.

He then asked Mehtaji to bring his son for whom a seat was provided facing the *prohit*. The Guru took his seat, his eyes sparkling with amusement. There was something about his sweet gentle face which attracted the eyes of all the assembled guests.

Hardyal began by propitiating the stars by chanting mantras in Sanskrit, and then he blessed the boy by reciting Veda Mantras and blessed the sacred thread. He was about to place it round Guru Nanak's shoulder, when Guru Sahib stopped him.

" What is this cotton thread ? " he asked. " Why is it worn ?." " And what advantage does it confer on the wearer ? "

" This thread is a symbol of high lineage and spiritual inheritance " replied Hardyal.

" How is this thread made ? " asked Guru Sahib.

" Who makes it ? Does it not decay ? How does it absorb spiritual power ? "

Hardyal was confused, but answered : " It is made out of pure cotton. A Brahman makes it and endows it with the power of Mantras. When it decays, it is replaced by a new one."

" Why, may I ask, are goats killed and feasts given ? " asked the Guru.

" Your father is a Kshatriya and his relations are Kshatriyas and it is lawful for them to eat meat," replied the Pandit.

The Guru raised his large luminous eyes and said :—

> What strange ceremony is this ?
> The Brahman spins a thread out of cotton
> And twists it into shape.
> When it decays a new one takes its place.
> If the thread had any virtue
> It would not decay or break.
> They kill goats without mercy
> And prepare a feast
> And guests clamour for more and more.

Thus saying, the Guru rose from his seat and turned to the assembled guests and spoke sweetly :

My elders worthy of all respect,
Is it not strange
That he who performs the ceremony
And claims to foretell the future
Charges a fee for the performance ?
He places no control on his senses
Nor protects his beard from spit of greed
He puts no restraint on his eyes or tongue,
On his hands and feet.
In all actions, he is unrestrained
And yet he puts a twisted thread
Round the neck of others.
Hear, O men, this strange phenomenon—
The man with a blind mind claims to be enlightened.

The Guru then turned towards the Pandit, " I will not wear this thread. It is no more sacred than the cotton from which it is spun."

The whole assembly was struck dumb. They all tried to persuade him but the Guru refused to be persuaded.

The Pandit in utter despair then asked, " What kind of sacred thread, O Nanak, wouldst thou wear ? "

The Guru said :—

Out of the cotton of compassion
Spin the thread of contentment,
Tie knots of continence, give it the twist of truth.
Make such a sacred thread for the mind,
Such a thread once worn will never break
Nor get soiled burnt or lost.
The man who weareth such a thread
Is blessed.
Thou buyest a thread for a pice
And seated in a plastered square
Putteth it round the neck of others.
Claiming an inheritance of holiness
Thy thread helps neither here nor hereafter.
The wearer dieth and leaves it behind.

The audience was hushed into silence, the truth of what the Guru said could not be disputed. They all felt that the regalia of sanctity without inner conversion was like dressing a freebooter in garments of holiness. They were for the time overpowered by the truth and irresistible influence of the true teacher.

His father, however, under the spell of conventional religion, was deeply disappointed at the behaviour of his son in refusing to put on the sacred thread and discarding the ancient custom prescribed by Hindu scriptures for all twice-born castes.

3

MEHTA KALU, LIKE ALL FATHERS, WAS ANXIOUS TO LEAD HIS SON along the path which he himself had found profitable. He could not reconcile himself to his son cultivating unworldliness and abstaining from taking any interest in occupations which he regarded as useful. He kept him under close observation and discovered that he cared for animals, enjoyed feeding them and making friends with them. He also noticed that he preferred to spend his days out in the fields sitting under trees and enjoyed being out-of-doors.

This gave him an idea that he could interest the Guru in becoming a stock-breeder.

One day he approached the Guru. " You seem very fond of cows and buffaloes and their calves. "

" I am," said the Guru. " They cannot ask what they want so I like to give them what they need."

" How do you know ? " asked the father.

" By sympathy and understanding," replied the Guru.

" They have, like us, hunger not only of the body but also of the soul."

Mehta Kalu did not like the drift of conversation and suddenly suggested, " If you are so fond of animals, why don't you take out a herd to graze ? "

" Nothing would please me better," said the Guru, " for then I could see them well-fed."

Next day the Guru took a small herd out. The cows and buffaloes followed him as if they had been attached to him for a long time. He brought them home in the evening.

One day the Guru took the herd out and then sat under a tree and soon passed into deep meditation unaware of things around him. His cattle strayed into a neighbouring field and feasted on the growing crop. Just as they had almost finished grazing, the owner of the field appeared and saw the result of his labour in ruin. He turned from his field to the Guru and said, " Wake up, you sluggard, see what your cattle have done. They have ruined my crop. How am I and my family to live ? "

The Guru looked up with eyes full of compassion, and said, " Have patience, your field will give you a greater return than you have ever harvested."

" You cannot deceive me by words," he said. " I am going to Rai Bular and I will make your father pay the full value of the crop." Enraged beyond measure, shouting and complaining, he ran to the village.

The Guru fixed his eyes full of nectar on the ruined crop and the whole field smiled back a green and luxuriant crop.

The owner approached Rai Bular and in bitterness of heart told him of his loss.

" Don't wax wrath," said Rai Bular. " I will send an appraiser with you who will estimate the loss and I will see that you are fully compensated."

Rai Bular gave instructions and the owner accompanied by the appraiser came to the field. The appraiser was no friend of Mehta Kalu. He thought that he would get even with him and assess heavy damages. They were astonished when they reached the field to find it lush with the growing crop.

The appraiser began to upbraid the owner of the field. " Have you no eyes ? Were you sun-struck not to see that your crop was all right ? "

The owner could not believe his eyes. He touched the crop with his own hand and held down his head, and said, " What can I say ? A miracle has happened. My eyes did not deceive me. I was in full possession of my senses. I saw what I saw."

The appraiser returned to Rai Bular and told him that all was well with the crop. Rai Bular had heard of Nanak and his discourse to his teacher and his refusal to wear the sacred thread. He was confirmed in his belief that Nanak was a man of God.

A few days later, Rai Bular himself saw an astonishing scene. He was returning from an adjoining village, when, from a distance, he saw Nanak sleeping in a field and a cobra holding his hood over his head, while all the cattle sat round him. Rai Bular thought the boy was bitten and was dead, as he was lying absolutely motionless. Rai Bular approached the spot hurriedly. As he reached the spot, the cobra disappeared and Nanak got up and greeted him with a smile. Rai Bular was so moved that he immediately jumped down from his horse, embraced the Guru and kissed him. From that day onward Rai Bular never failed or faltered in upholding the young Nanak who, he believed, was a messenger of God.

4

THE STORY OF THE GRAZING OF THE FIELD DULY REACHED Mehta Kalu. He was deeply disturbed and decided he could no more trust his son with the care of his cows and buffaloes. He had an anxious talk with his wife and both decided to take a firm stand with the Guru and put him in some profession for which he expressed a liking. Father and mother lovingly called the Guru one day and opened the subject.

" I am old," said the father, " and may pass away any day to the other world." " You have to take my place. Your mother will have to depend on you. You must no more idle away your days but must do something useful."

" Father, if you are aware that you may have to leave this earth," said the Guru, " what preparations are you making to secure happiness in the other world ? "

Mehta Kalu held his breath ; he could not give an appropriate answer.

" It is not propitious to talk of such things " said his mother.

This gave time to Mehta Kalu to recover, and he added there is plenty of time to think of the other world. We should think of the world in which we live. " If you do not do something in this world, you will be bankrupt here and go empty-handed to the other. Now listen, I have a small area of land. why don't you start farming on it ?"

" Father, I am all the time engaged in real farming," said the Guru. Listen

This body is the field
The mind is the ploughman
Modesty the irrigating water.
I sow the seed of the Divine Name
And with the leveller of contentment
Pulverise the crust of pride into true humility.
In it the seed of love will prosper.
Seated in the abode of truth
I behold its progress
Father, Mammon accompanieth not man
The world is deluded by it.
Only few walk out of the delusion and attain discrimination."

His father refused to give any heed to the Guru's homily and continued : " If farming does not appeal to you, why not open a shop ? " The Guru again answered :

" I make this frail body my shop
I make meditation the container
I stock it with the true name
I trade with the dealers of the true name
And thus accumulate the wealth of truth.

His father remained unconvinced and pressed him to become a dealer in horses. The Guru answered him again in another parable :

" He is a true dealer in horses
Who breeds the horses of truth,
Stores wealth of virtue
To meet the needs of the way,
And worries no more,
Full of unfailing faith
That in the abode of the Formless
He shall share its bliss."

Kalu was now in despair, but he persisted in pressing on Nanak the need of doing something. " If you are not ready to take to business, then you had better take up an official position. I have some influence and can easily arrange it for you." The Guru replied :

" I serve my Master ;
You too should serve Him
With thy whole heart

With thy passions subdued,
Perform action with His Name in thy heart :
When He looks on thee with favour
Thy face will shine with fourfold splendour
Thou shalt be greatly blessed."

Having said this the Guru passed into a trance.

5

AS GURU NANAK GREW IN YEARS, HE STUDIOSULY AVOIDED company and sought seclusion. He would remain for long hours in his room abstaining from food and speech. He was now in his sixteenth year but had nothing in common with boys of his age. His face glowed with joy but his body suffered—so much so that his mother was greatly concerned about his health. Her friends shook their heads and told her that the poor boy was not normal, others said he was possessed by spirits. His parents tried their very best, but the Guru refused to give any explanation or to alter his ways.

Mehta Kalu at last decided to consult the best physicians in the neighbourhood. He invited Hari Dass, a well-known Vaidya and conducted him to Nanak's room. Hari Dass quietly sat himself down near Nanak and began to feel his pulse. The Guru withdrew his arm and said :

They have sent for you, O physician,
To discover my disease.
Thou hast put thy hand on my pulse
Simpleton ! Thou knowest it not
That the pain lies deep
In the region of the heart.
Thou couldst act as a physician
If thou canst first remove thine own disease.
The pain that disturbs thy peace
Then thou mayst diagnose the disease of others
And call thyself a physician."

Hari Dass smiled sardonically. He was familiar with cases of deranged mind.

" So you think I too am sick and need a cure ? "

" Undoubtedly," said the Guru, "you suffer from sickness of the soul."

" What is that sickness ? " asked Hari Dass.

The Guru looked at him with eyes full of compassion and said, " I-amness " is the disease. It separates us not only from our fellow-men, but from the source of life, God Himself."

" What are its symptoms ? " Hari Dass asked.

The Guru answered :

" Separation is a constant source of pain,
Hunger for union another,

The fear of the body perishing with disease,
And the haunting fear of myrmidons of death."

Hari Dass was lost in wonder for what the Guru said was true. He felt a strange peace stealing over him filling his heart and soul.

"You speak of the things of the spirit." "My concern is with the body alone."

The .Guru turned his loving eyes on him, and said, "Is body worth anything without the spirit ?" Just as—

Sandal wood is valued only
While it exhales perfume,
The body is valued
While it pulsates with life :
It is cast away,
When breath leaves it,
Then thy medicines are of no use.

"That is true," said the physician, "but how is it that this truth eludes mankind ?"

"Listen," said the Guru :

"Man's mind blind with desire,
Sows the seed of its own suffering,
In pursuit of indulgence of the self,
It forgets God and undergoes endless suffering.
O ! Ignorant physician,
Thy physic is of no avail :
Suffering itself is the symptom of disease,
As well as its cure."

"Is there no help ? Is there no way of effecting a cure ?" asked Hari Dass.

"Yes," said the Guru, "disease and its cause can be cured ·

By the saving grace of true name.
The bright and radiant name
Of the Infinite, when it fills the mind
Banishes its impurities,
And transmutes it into pure gold."

Hari Dass forgot all his professional ways and his task of curing Nanak. He sat spell-bound trying to draw into his soul the aroma of spirit which pervaded the Guru and when he left, it was as a disciple of the True Teacher. He told Mehta Kalu that his anxiety about his son was useless, as he was a teacher and destined to follow the way of all prophets.

6

MEHTA KALU IN SPITE OF ACCUMULATING EVIDENCE about the spiritual greatness of the Guru saw in him only a wayward boy, self-willed and headstrong who was wasting his days in profitless contemplation.

He would hold himself in patience for some days and then again devise some new way of interesting the Guru in learning the ways of the world.

One day he approached Guru Nanak, lovingly patted him on the back and said, " My son ! when will you learn to make honest and profitable bargains ? "

" Any time you command me to, father," replied Guru Nanak with a smile.

Mehta Kalu was pleased and counted out twenty rupees which he handed to his son. " Take this money," he said, " and go to the nearest market with your friend Bala and buy something in the cheapest market and sell it at the highest price. This is the way to make real profit. You must come back before sunset."

The Guru obeyed and with his friend Bala started for the neighbouring town. The Guru, however, left the public road taking a short-cut through uninhabited and unfrequented parts. He had not gone very far, when he saw a party of ascetics seated under a grove of trees. Guru Nanak went straight to them and bowing before the leader, who occupied a central place, sat near him and asked, " Why have you taken your abode in a deserted place ? "

" It may appear a deserted place to you," replied the leader. " But it is free from the shadow of evil places from where you come."

" Our needs are few," he continued. " We do not require all that the people in towns and villages require, and God in His mercy provides for us as He provides for all."

" Pardon my asking you, but when did you have your last meal ? " asked the Guru.

The leader smiled. " Some five days ago," he said. " Look at my companions. Do they reveal any signs of over-feeding ? It is well to acquire control over the appetites of the body."

" Does control over the appetite of the body gives control over the mind ?" asked the Guru.

" No, but it is the preliminary to effecting the control of the mind," replied the leader.

This pleased the Guru and he thought nothing could be more profitable than to feed these good men who were hungry. He took out twenty rupees in spite of the protests of Bala and placed the money before the leader.

" My boy ! take away this money which your father has given you for some other purpose. I have vowed never to touch money, but only cooked or uncooked food."

" It is a good principle," said the Guru. " I will go and fetch you some food."

The Guru immediately rose and with Bala went to the nearest bazar and purchased provisions which Bala thought were being purchased for a profitable transaction. Bala carried the purchases for him. On their way home, however, they again came across the party of ascetics sitting still without food.

The Guru stopped and without a moment's hesitation laid before the leader all his purchases and without waiting for a reply started homeward followed by Bala.

Guru Nanak stopped near a clump of a trees in the neighbourhood of his village and told Bala to go home. Bala obeyed. He met Mehta Kalu, just as he entered the village, who asked him where his son was. Bala told him that he had left him near the village grove.

" Take me there," commanded Mehta Kalu.

Bala led him to the spot where he had left the Guru ; they found him seated calmly, lost in meditation.

Mehta Kalu shook him angrily, and said, " What are you doing here ? What have you done with the money ? "

The Guru opened his eyes and looked him full in the face but made no answer.

Mehta Kalu grew still more angry and was about to slap him, when Rai Bular, the owner of the village, appeared on the scene.

Mehta Kalu greeted him and said," I am in a great distress. I gave my son twenty rupees this morning to go to the town and make some profit. He has wasted all the money and returned empty-handed."

" How has the money been wasted ? " enquired Rai Bular, turning to Bala who was trembling with fear.

" Forgive me, sir," said Bala. " The Guru bought some provisions with the money and, finding a party of ascetics who had gone without food for many days, in spite of my protests he gave it to them."

" Why did you do it ? " asked Rai Bular.

" I could think of no more honest and more profitable bargain," said the Guru, " My investment will bless the giver here and hereafter."

Rai Bular was a man of real understanding. He turned to Mehta Kalu and said, " Your son is not meant for gaining this world ; his gains are gains of Heaven. Don't grow angry with him but let him follow his own way, for his way is the right way."

Kalu could say nothing. He bowed his head to Rai Bular, though he remained entirely unconvinced.

The Guru went straight to his room and sat down. He would neither talk nor take any food. His mother hovered round him.

" My son ! " she pleaded, " you must eat something, otherwise how can you live without food ? My son, I do not understand all this. What is this true Name of which you so constantly speak ? "

The Guru said :

" To remember Him is to live
To forget Him is to die.
It is difficult to expound
The true Name.

When hunger for it
Awakens in the heart
All other hungers depart
And this hunger consumes all suffering.
O my mother !
The true Lord
How can He be named
He Whose Name is Truth ?
The greatness of His true Name
Men's mind weary trying to grasp :
Their collective efforts are in vain.
His greatness cannot be over-stated.
Nor His greatness under-estimated.
He does not die nor is He mourned.
He is the giver,
The flow of His gifts is unending.

"How can one know Him ?," asked the mother.

He replied :

" There is only this to know
There is no one but He
Neither in the past
Nor in the future
He Who created the day
And then created the night
His bounties are as boundless as He Himself.

" But they say that only the great Pandits can approach Him ? " said his mother.

The Guru smiled and said :

"They alone are of low birth
Who forget the true Master
Without the grace of His Name
Their status is low :—
There is no other distinction.

The mother and son continued to talk for a long time. The link of love drew him to his mother and he partook of the food which she placed before him and then, as if a new chord had been touched, he chanted hymns in praise of God.

7

BIBI NANKI, THE MARRIED SISTER OF THE GURU, CAME TO visit her parents with her husband, Jai Ram, who was Dewan of Nawab Daulat Khan Lodhi. She was devoted to her younger brother and noticed with concern his drift towards unworldliness and her father's impatience at the boy's indifference towards all that he valued most : position, wealth and worldly prosperity.

She talked it over with her husband and her mother and decided to take her brother to her home and to get him a regular position in the Nawab's service. She approached her father with the proposal and he said, " You will spoil him with your love and encourage him to be idle."

" No, father," she said, " I am hoping that regular work will draw him to the daily needs of life and then I will arrange his marriage and, when he has a wife to support, he will no longer be so disdainful of money."

" You seem to be right but I must consult my master, who takes such a deep interest in my son." Accordingly he explained his daughter's plan to Rai Bular, who agreed with a smile and said, " Your son has a light which will guide others wherever he goes."

The day for Nanki's departure was fixed and the Guru readily agreed to go with his sister. Rai Bular gave a banquet in his honour and the whole village came to see him off.

Rai Bular before saying good-bye took the Guru aside and said, " Tell me if I can be of any service to you."

" Yes," said the Guru, " render true service to all the creatures of God, relieve the heavy-laden, bring the balm of sympathy to lacerated hearts, combine justice with mercy, and if at any moment thy own power availeth not, lift thy mind to God and pray for His mercy."

Rai Bular was more than ever struck by the advice of the Guru and bowed with great affection and respect.

8

THE GURU WAS IN HIS SEVENTEENTH YEAR, WHEN HE CAME to stay with his sister. His brother-in-law brought him an offer of the post of store-keeper to the Nawab. He raised no objection but took up his duty with a regularity which was an agreeable surprise to his sister. After a time, this encouraged his sister to arrange his marriage. The Guru raising no objection, he was married in due course and lived in a separate house with his wife and his two old friends, Bala and Mardana. Both Bala and Mardana lived to serve the Guru and remained with him to the end.

For three years, the Guru lived the life of a householder and his wife gave birth to two sons, who were afterwards known as great ascetics. It seemed as if it was the purpose of the Guru to demonstrate that the house-hold was a school in which self-love is changed into love for others and that to earn an honest living was a pre-requisite of godliness.

The post of store-keeper was a great responsibility. The State collected all its dues in kind and stored them in granaries and all payments were made in grain after providing reserves to meet the requirements of bad years. Only the surplus was sold.

The Guru performed his duties freely with a diligence which surprised his sister and brother-in-law. He gave to all who asked for grain according to their need and yet the granaries were full. In course of three years a volume of opinion grew which constantly impressed on the Nawab that his store-keeper was recklessly giving away the grain and he would find his granaries empty. They said that when weighing out he reached 'taira' (thirteen) which means 'thine' he so lost himself that he went on repeating 'thine' 'I am thine,' 'I am thine' and emptied his scales. They said that the store-house had become the gathering place of beggars and poor people, whom the store-keeper fed at the cost of the Nawab.

The Nawab ordered an enquiry which was conducted with great care. Accounts were scrutinised; grain was reweighed. His detractors were surprised when the stores were found full and accounts showed a balance in favour of the Guru.

The Guru, however, sent in his resignation. "Why have you sent your resignation?" asked Jai Ram.

"My account is closed," said the Guru, "and with it my first mission has come to a close."

"What is your mission?" asked Jai Ram.

"To bring men nearer to God to enjoy the treasures of happiness," said the Guru.

"Where are the treasures of happiness in this world of woe?" asked Jai Ram.

"They are within you," said the Guru. "But alas! it is the pomp and glory of the world, the puppet play of passion which cheats man of his heritage and rewards him with suffering."

"Is renunciation of the world the way?" asked Jai Ram. "Are you going to be a *Sanyasi*?"

"No, my brother. Have I not married and begotten sons; have I not lived the life of a householder? No, I am not going to be a *Sanyasi*, but show the way which every householder can follow for the freedom of the soul," said the Guru.

"Can you show me the way?" asked Jai Ram.

The Guru replied, "Have I not shown it everyday that I have lived with you? Now I will proclaim it to the world; I must go."

"So your mind is made up," said Jai Ram. "What am I to tell your father and mother?"

"Tell them I am doing the work of Him Who is the father of all creation and my work will bring peace and comfort to them as to others."

He turned to go. His wife clung to his feet. "In whose care are you leaving me?" she sobbed through her tears.

" In the care of Him Who cares for all," he said and with these words, he put his hand on her head and her despair was changed into calm content.

" Go, my lord and master," she said, bowing. " The world is in flames, go and quench its fire."

The Guru then left his home.

9

THE GURU WENT OUT AND SAT ON THE BANK OF THE RIVER in Samadhi. As the Guru closed his eyes, it seemed to him as if spirit of Kalyug trembled at the appearance of the saviour and let all its fury rage round the Guru. Thunder, lightning and myriads of formless frightful shapes robed in blackness crowded round him sharpening their five-pointed weapons of passion, anger, greed, delusion and conceit, emitting flames of Trihsna (desire) and wielding the doubled-bladed sword of hate and harmfulness. He let them pass and remained calm like a lotus amidst stormy waters.

Then there passed before his mind palaces and pleasure houses flowing with milk and honey and swarming with maidens of unsurpassed beauty. The Guru smiled and said :

> Pearl-built peerless palaces
> Adorned with precious gems
> Fragrant with all the scents of earth—
> These delude fools who forget His name
> Who have not Him in their hearts
> My Master had told me
> There is no other place like His.

Then there passed before his eyes the richness of earth and all the treasured wealth that lies hid under sea and mountains. The Guru again smiled and said :

> Were earth blazing with diamonds,
> And sparkling with rubies,
> Overflowing with maidens of glamorous beauty,
> These delude only the fools.
> Who have not Him in their hearts.

Then, it seemed to him that the kingdom of earth was at his feet. He again smiled and said :

> What does it matter if I become a king,
> And command mighty armies,
> And occupy a golden throne,
> And like the wind my commands encompass the earth ?
> These delude fools only
> Who have not Him in their hearts.

Then it seemed as if he was tempted by the offer of supernatural powers and sovereignty over nature, but he rejected these with the remark,

If I exercise supernatural powers
And can create wealth at a gesture
Can appear and disappear at will
And thus win popular respect—
These delude fools only
Who have not Him in their hearts.

The Guru discarded with scorn all that the earth and heavens could offer and with his mind calm as that of a pellucid lake, he lost himself in contemplation and became one with the Supreme.

Next morning people said they saw him walking straight into the stream and disappear entirely from human sight. It was held that he was drowned and his sister and brother-in-law in deep distress searched the river in vain for his body.

The Guru, however, had ascended to the plane of truth and appeared before the True One. On the third day he reappeared with a luminous halo round his face. Crowds gathered round him. He then uttered the first article of his faith. In a state of trance he chanted :

Where is the door to thy dwelling-place
Seated wherein thou controllest all
Where many musicians play on their instruments
And innumerable songsters raise their voices
And celestial musicians make divine music
And fire and water sing thy praise.
Also the king of Justice,
Also the recording angel of deeds (good and evil)
Who records in the light of Dharma,
Also the Ishwar, the Brahma and the Goddess
Adorned with Immortality
Also Indra seated on his throne
With his host of angels,
They sing hymns of praise at thy door.
Also *sidhas* and *sadhus* in their contemplations and trances,
And ascetics and devotees of truth,
And selfless and fearless warriors,
The Pandits and the learned men
Who recite Vedas,
And lovely enchantresses of heart
In high heavens and lower regions
Sing thy praises.
The valuable gems of thy creation
And sixty-eight sacred pools and rivers,
The most powerful warriors
And the four sources of production
Sing thy praises.

The spheres, also the globes and the worlds created
And supported by thee
Sing thy praises
Many others sing whom I cannot recall.
But thy devotees,
Who win thy grace,
Imbued with thy love,
Adore thee, they are,
The true devotees of the eternal master.

Then he pronounced the first principle of his creed :

The one Aum (Ik onkar)
The true Word
The creative spirit
Free of fear and hate
Timeless, birthless, self-existent
Known by the grace of the true teacher
Repeat (the true Name)
True in the beginning
True in all ages
Who is true and who shall be true.

And he continued speaking as if from a far-away plane :

He is True and His Name is true
He is and He shall be
He who has arranged
This play of the Universe
This material world,
In various forms and hues.
He shall never pass away.
He enjoys the sight of His own artistry,
To His own Eternal Glory.
He is the all-powerful,
Subject to no other command.
He is the Lord of lords, the King of kings,
All live under His will.

In a state of ecstasy, he continued :

Thou art all wisdom, omniscent,
Deeper than the oceans,
How could a fish ascertain,
The limits of an ocean.
Thou art everywhere,
Wherever I look,
There art Thou.

Separated from Thee,
Like a fish I die.
I know not the fisherman (the angel of death)
I know not the noose of his net.
I am aware of only one thing,
He is everywhere,
He is not far away,
All acts are performed,
In His presence.
He seeth all.
Men forget to serve Him
Or to remember His Name.
They enjoy what He gives.
There is no door but His door
Nanak the suppliant says
My soul and body are His sacrifice.

Then raising his eyes, he pronounced an Invocation :

Thou art near, thou art far
Thou art all in all
Thou seest, Thou heareth
Thou createth this Universe
What pleaseth Thee
That is the only right action.

Thus imbued with the spirit of God, the Guru turned towards the town again to kindle the heart of others with the love of God which filled his own, and overflowed.

10

THE GURU THEN WALKED TO THE CREMATION GROUND AND took his seat in a dreary spot. Men and women came to see him and passed kind and unkind remarks. Some said a ghost had taken hold of him and others said that he was out of his mind. The Guru said :

Foolish people think ghosts have possessed me
Others with pity pronounce my name.
They little know of God-intoxication.
Nanak is possessed with the love of God and nothing else.

Jai Ram was deeply distressed. He consulted a Moulvi who was held in great esteem. The Moulvi said he would cure Nanak and exercise the evil spirit. He came and sat down in front of the Guru and began his incantations. The Guru turned to him and said :

They whose crop is ruined in the field
What can they gather on the threshing floor ?
Accursed are they who write and sell God's Name.

The Moulvi, however, continued asking the spirit that possessed Nanak to declare itself. The Guru laughed and said :

This foolish world thinks
He in whose heart
Dwells fear of God
Who acknowledges
No other but Him
Who submits to His will
Is mad.
Is this the mark of wisdom ?

" You talk like a Pandit," said the Moulvi, " but you act like a fool."

" How do you reconcile the two ? " asked the Guru. " You consider me mad because I regard as valueless what men like you value."

He
Whose heart is filled
With the love of the Lord
Who considers himself
Less than the dust
And all others his betters—
Can such a one lack sanity ?

" So you are sane and I believe it," said the Moulvi. " Your abnormal behaviour is not due to any external cause but your own will. What is your purpose in abandoning your home ? "

The Guru got up and declared, " To serve mankind, there is no Hindu, there is no Muslim."

The Moulvi turned to Jai Ram and said, "There is nothing wrong with Nanak."

Jai Ram gave him a rupee and he departed. In the meanwhile Nanki and Guru's wife arrived. " Dear brother," said Nanki, " why have you abandoned your home, wife and sons and taken your residence in this dreadful place ? "

" Is not this the place where eventually everybody must come ? " the Guru replied. " I have come to it of my own sweet will instead of on the shoulders of other men. They indeed are foolish who ignore the truth that this mortal body must perish."

Nanki again appealed to her brother to think of his family and not leave them.

The Master replied, " My dear sister, humanity is my family and in serving it I serve you also."

The news that the Guru had disappeared and appeared again and also that he has said, " There is no Hindu and no Musalman " reached the Nawab.

The Qazi demanded that the Guru should be summoned and required to explain his sweeping assertion which, the Qazi said, bordered on heresy.

" He could say what he wished about his own religion, but he had no right to talk lightly of Islam " he added.

A messenger was accordingly deputed to bring the Guru to the Court of the Nawab. The messenger approached the Guru but he was so overwhelmed by the spirit of peace pervading the Guru that he humbly submitted, " Sir, the Nawab shall be very pleased if you grace his Court with your presence."

The Guru answered, " My brother, I have no concern with the Nawab now. I am in the service of Him, who is the Sovereign of this whole World."

The messenger returned and reported the conversation. The Qazi himself rose angrily and said, " I will bring this heretic myself to your presence."

The Qazi, as he approached the Guru, seemed to lose mastery over self and in spite of his resolution respectfully said, " Nanak, come with me ; the Nawab is anxious to be enlightened by you."

" If he seeks light, I cannot refuse the summons " said the Guru and accompanied him.

The Nawab was a great believer in saints. Nanak's administration of his store, his disappearance and appearance had greatly impressed him. He rose to receive the Guru and gave him a seat next to himself.

" I am puzzled," he said, " by your alleged pronouncement that there is no Hindu and no Musalman. Is not Qazi Sahib a true Musalman ? Am I not an humble follower of the Prophet ? "

" Nawab Sahib, it is very difficult indeed to be a Musalman " said the Guru.

The Qazi turned on him with flashing eyes and said, " What do you mean ? "

The Guru answered, as was his wont, in a hymn :

He who is firm in his faith
Has a right to be called a Muslim.
His acts must accord with his faith in the Prophet
He must clean his heart of pride and greed
No more troubled by the two impostors—life and death.
Resigned to the will of God
Knowing Him as the Doer
Freed from the domination of the self
Compassionate to all things
Such a one may call himself a Muslim.

The Qazi was not prepared to accept the verdict and asked, " What are you ? "

" I am neither a Muslim nor a Hindu," answered the Guru.

" Why ? " asked the Qazi.

The Guru said, " Only he has a right to call himself religious, who lives in the light of God's word brought to earth by prophets of all religions. To me all religions are His."

The time for offering prayers had come, so the Nawab intervened, " If all religions are the same to you, will you join us in offering prayers ?"

" With pleasure," answered the Guru, " if you or the Qazi will lead the prayer."

The Nawab and the Qazi rose and the Guru accompanied them.

The news spread like wild fire that Nanak had entered the mosque to offer prayers with the Nawab. Nanak's sister and wife, Jai Ram and other Hindus were much perturbed. They thought Nanak was about to be converted. They all rushed to the mosque where Nanak was to offer Namaz and waited at its gates.

It was Friday and a big congregation of Muslims had assembled ; the Qazi stood first, behind him the Nawab and then Nanak and other prominent persons and behind them the rest of the people. When Namaz was offered and the faithful kneeled, Nanak was observed to remain standing and taking no part in the prayers.

When the Namaz was over, the Qazi in an angry mood turned to Nanak, "You are an impostor," he said. " You said you will pray with us and you remained standing."

" I promised to offer Namaz under your leadership," said Nanak. " Since you were not praying, how could I ?"

The Qazi turned to the Nawab. " Have you ever heard such blasphemy ?" he said.

The Nawab turned to the Guru : " What is your explanation ? " he enquired.

" Now tell me, does Namaz merely consist in kneeling and bowing ?" enquired the Guru.

" No," said the Qazi. " It is merely the outer expression of humility."

The Guru said, " Then tell me what is the inner expression ?"

The Qazi replied, " The worship that the spirit offers in terms of the words of prayers."

" That is why I said, neither you nor the Nawab were praying, for while your body was bowing your spirit was occupied with other things—both yours and that of the Nawab," said the Guru.

" What things ? " said the Qazi angrily.

The Guru said, " You were thinking of your mare which had just foaled and you were afraid lest the foal may fall into the well which is in your courtyard. Am I right ? "

The Qazi held down his head for it was true.

" And me ? " asked the Nawab humbly.

" Your thoughts were not rising up to God," said the Guru. " You were absorbed in thoughts of horses, which your agents are purchasing in Qandhar."

The Nawab bowed and said the Guru was right and the whole congregation was struck dumb with amazement.

The Guru then turned to the congregation. " I will tell you how to offer prayers and follow the holy script of the Quran :

In the Mosque of love
Spread the carpet of faith,
Enjoy only your rightful earnings,
Follow the holy script.
Make restraint and modesty thy circumcision,
Moderation thy fast,
Right action thy pilgrimage to Kaba.
Make truth thy spiritual guide,
Good works thy creed,
Thus become a Muslim
Repeat His Name on thy rosary
He will exalt thee.

Listen, O people ! I speak the truth. Learn to realise the meaning of prayers, purify your minds that the words may acquire power and become significant.

The five periods of the day
Are associated with five prayers
And they have five separate names.
Their first requirement is truthfulness.
The second to live on lawful earning.
The third to give in God's name.
The fourth to discipline the mind
With right resolution.
And the fifth to praise God.
He whose deeds precede the word of prayer
Has the right to call himself a Muslim :
They wander into the wilderness of untruth
Who follow the form and ignore the spirit."

Then the Guru turned to go. The Nawab asked him to stay but the Guru said that it was time for him to carry out the commands of his Master :

" I must follow the path ordained for me."

After taking his leave of the Nawab he returned home to say good-bye to his wife, sister and other relatives.

" Where are you going ? " they asked.

" I am going to serve my Master," he said, standing in the courtyard. " Wherever He bids me there I go."

The Guru cast his eyes full of love on the members of his family and their distress was changed into good cheer. Then, when they were all at peace, the Guru quietly walked out.

11

THE GURU LEFT SULTANPUR ACCOMPANIED BY BALA AND Mardana. They had not gone far when the Guru turned to Mardana and said, " Go to the North and meet a friend and receive from him a Rubab which is yours."

" But, Sir," said Mardana, " I know no friend and have never played on the Rubab."

The Guru looked at him with light of love in his eyes and said, " Do as I tell you and discover for yourself the truth of what I am saying."

The kindly eye that met Mardana convinced him that the Guru was not trifling with his credulity. He immediately obeyed and proceeded in the direction which the Guru had indicated to him. He had just crossed a hedge when an old man with white beard and bright beautiful face greeted him and enquired, " What are you looking for ? "

" I am looking for some one who is waiting for me." And what do you want from him ? " the old man asked.

" A Rubab," said Mardana.

" So Nanak Nirankari has sent you," said the old man. " Tell him Farenda, his servant, has carried out his command. Blessed are they who have the privilege of his divine company. Here is the Rubab, which I have carried for you for long years."

Mardana grasped the beautiful instrument and turned in gratitude to Farenda to find that he had disappeared.

Mardana took the Rubab and returned to the Guru marvelling at the miracle.

" Now take up the Rubab and play," said the Guru.

" I have never played, Sir," he pleaded.

" You were a master player," said the Guru, " and once you run your fingers over it, your skill will come back to you in a flash."

Mardana obeyed ; his fingers began to move automatically and poured forth divine music. The Guru accompanied him by a hymn :

If I live millions of years
On air alone
Sun and moon
No more mark the time
I could not even then describe Thy greatness
Though the changeless
Thou the formless
Men speak of Thee
Within the limits of their power
If there were millions
Of maunds of paper
And ink without end

And a pen driven by the wind
Even then thy greatness
Could not be expressed
How can I exalt Thy Name ?

12

THE GURU PASSED INTO A STATE OF BLISS. IT WAS NEARLY sunset when he started on his journey again with the Muslim minstrel and the Hindu attendant who symbolised his own catholicity of spirit.

The Indian social system was in a state of dissolution. Man recognised no social bond of unity with one another. No one thought of protecting and promoting the common weal beyond one's own interest.

The result was that a potentially powerful people were powerless to resist tyranny and secure for themselves their ordinary needs. Conditions have not very much improved to-day. The Guru aimed at the regeneration of society by kindling in the hearts of Hindus and Muslims alike the spirit of truth and its fruit—a feeling of brotherhood and a complete disregard of forms which divided brother from brother. He held up to ridicule practices which were no more tenable and old institutions which were no longer helpful.

The Guru halted at Saidapur, now known as Emenabad, and lodged at the house of a carpenter named Lalu, a poor man, who lived by the sweat of his labour. Lalu welcomed the Guru with great humility and reverence.

It happened that Malik Bhago, the Dewan of the Pathan Governor, was giving a sacrificial feast and expected all religions and holy men to join and partake of his repast to enable him to acquire merit.

The news that a saint was staying at the house of Lalu reached Malik Bhago. He immediately sent a servant to invite the Guru along with his followers. The Guru, however, refused to accept the invitation. Bhago believed that his 'yag' would be incomplete unless all the holy men graced his house. He sent his man repeatedly to bring the Guru. The Guru went to his house.

Bhago said, "You are a strange man : you can eat the food cooked by a Shudra."

"I have no caste," said the Guru, "nor do I sit in a chauka to eat : for me the whole earth is pure."

"Then why did you refuse to join my feast ?" said Bhago in a sarcastic voice.

"Do you really want to know ?" the Guru asked.

"Yes" said Bhago.

"Give me some food cooked for distribution at your house," said the Guru.

The Guru asked Lalu also to fetch some food from his house. In the meanwhile a great crowd had gathered round the Guru including the Nawab himself. When the food from the two houses was brought, Lalu brought a piece of bread made of barley flour. The Guru took the piece which came from the house of Lalu and some rich food which came from Bhago's house in his right and left hand respectively and squeezed the two. From Lalu's food oozed out drops of milk and from that of Bhago drops of blood.

" Now you see why I refused to eat your food," said the Guru. "Your food is blood-stained and drawn from others. Lalu enjoys what he earns by hard labour and shares his earnings with others. No sanctified *chauka* can make your food pure."

Bhago fell at the feet of the Guru and prayed for mercy. The Nawab also bowed in all humility before the Guru.

" Listen," said the Guru :

That which belongs to another
Is unlawful like the flesh of a pig
To a Musalman and cow's flesh to a Hindu.
The Guru and the Peer will extend their grace
If thou refrainest from eating carrion.
Carrion does not become lawful
By breathing God's name over it
Nor do we secure paradise
By indulgence in holy talk.
The fruit of false talk is falsehood
Only good deeds open the road to salvation.

The Guru stayed a day with Lalu. Men gathered round him as moths gather round a light. He instructed all those who gathered round him, thus, sowing the seed of Sikhism.

13

NEXT DAY THE GURU WALKED TO THE TOWN OF SIALKOT and, as he was passing through the street, he stopped at the shop of a grain dealer and began to examine his weights. The shopkeeper told him that each weight is measured. The Guru took up the smallest weight and raised it to his head, and said, " This measure is indeed blessed."

" Why ? " asked the crowd that had gathered round him.

The Guru said, " In its small and humble way it serves the need of the humble and the indigent. Blessed are the humble who have fear of God in their hearts for they are free from the sin of self-indulgence, and will learn to love God."

The grain dealer fell at the Guru's feet and humbly asked him to grace his house with his visit.

" Not now," said the Guru, "but I will come when your gains are no more contaminated with wrong dealing. A dealer in grain is the sustainer of life and must be honest and true in his dealings. When you become a true dealer and giver of food I will come to your house."

The Guru then walked out of the city and sat in a place away from all human habitation.

Mardana much puzzled asked, " Why do you prefer the wilderness to the comforts of the town ? "

" There is no comfort in a place where there is no truth," replied the Guru. "The air of the town is charged with hypocrisy. Who could breathe it with impunity ? "

Mardana pleaded that he was hungry and he could not live on the wild air that blew about him.

" Take this slip of paper," said the Guru. "Enter the city and show it to rich and poor alike. He who answers the questions which I have written on it will give you food." The Guru put two questions, "What is real ? What is unreal ? "

Mardana walked through the town showing his slip of paper to rich and poor alike. They refused to look at it and laughed at Mardana, till he reached the shop of a baker who took the paper and wrote a reply, "Death is real and living is unreal." Then he served Mardana with food. When Mardana had appeased his hunger, the baker asked him to take him to the person who had put the question. Mardana asked him to accompany him. The baker, when he saw the Guru, humbly bowed before him and asked, " Show me the true way, O thou searcher of hearts ! "

"Seek and you will find it. It is found by search and lost by discussion," said the Guru.

The baker was so impressed by the Guru that he accompanied him for many days, till the Guru ordered him to go back.

" I want to be a Faqir," pleaded the baker. " I wish to give up the world."

" Listen," said the Guru. " It is not by shirking our duty that we become saints, but by daily performance of that which is ordained. We learn the beginning of self-denial by denying ourselves for the sake of our family, by active sympathy, with suffering, and forbearance for all."

" Then why is it that people leave their hearths and homes in search of God ? " asked the baker.

" There are true seekers and selfish forsakers," said the Guru, " but my way is the way of rising by step steadily and surely by purification of the mind by daily conflict with the force that darkens the light of the soul. This is only possible if we do our day-to-day duty with the name of God on our lips, so that all our actions are performed in His service who is the Lord of all that exists."

The Guru then repeated the opening passage of Japji and said, " Meditate on this, try to reach at inner meaning, then the true desire in your heart will gain strength and you will become a devotee. The light of the beloved will illumine your innermost being. Remember renunciation of outward things does not make for inner righteousness. Words are meaningless till translated into action."

The baker repeated the opening passage of the Japji after the Guru and understood its meaning, and then took his leave of the Guru.

He returned to his shop, lived the life of a householder with the name of God on his lips animated by a spirit of service which made life a blessing for all. He became a friend of Hindus and Muslims alike. He saw God in the temple and in the mosque and found in the service of his fellow men, the truest method of worship.

14

THE GURU WANDERED FROM VILLAGE TO VILLAGE KINDLING hearts ready to receive the light with the torch of truth, irrespective of caste or creed. He came across a place where lived Sajjan (meaning a good friend) a notorious thief. Sajjan always dressed himself in pure white, wore the Hindu mark of sanctity on his forehead and displayed a Muslim rosary round his neck. He had built a Hindu temple and a Muslim mosque at his gate. He invited wayfarers to his residence and then robbed them. He was always on the watch for travellers and when he saw the Guru and his followers, he rejoiced for his victims looked innocent and incapable of defending themselves willingly. He invited them to his home. The Guru accepted his invitation with a sparkle of amusement in his eye.

When night fell the Guru asked Mardana to play the Rubab and he invited Sajjan to come and listen to his hymns. Sajjan agreed. Mardana touched the Rubab and as his fingers wandered over the strings music came that seemed to find its way to the heart of Sajjan. Then the Guru began his hymn :

Bronze is bright and shining
Rub it and it turns black
And a hundred washings cannot remove it.
They are Sajjans, they are true comrades
Whose friendship bears the mark of sincerity
Who are present in a friend's hour of need.
A peepal in the courtyard, a Dharamsala at the gate
Attractive in outer appearance but hollow within,
The red marks of sanctity on the forehead
And a rosary round the neck
Deceitful disguises to cheat the world.
Houses and mansions decorated and painted
They will be of little use ; they must crumble away.
Men clad in white like herons wait for their victims
At places of pilgrimage and follow a nefarious trade
They are not sajjans, they are not good friends
But like the seemal tree that attracts birds
By its brilliant flowers and is without fruit,
It sends them back hungry and unsatisfied.
So men without virtue are like a tree without fruit :
They blindly load themselves with sin
Knowing not that the road is long and dreary.

And those heavy-laden with sin
Have to traverse the dreary road
Blinded and without sight ; they cannot ascend the heights.
Labour, cunning and craft are of no avail
Nanak says remember God and find release from the prison-house of self.

Sajjan who was waiting to follow his nefarious calling listened and as he listened realised that the Guru's words were addressed to him and were entering his heart and demanding repentance. Sajjan was overwhelmed with consciousness of his misdeeds. There passed before his mind's eye a lurid picture of all that he had done. He fell at the Guru's feet. "I have sinned grievously, O True Teacher ! " he said. " Save me for you are the saviour."

Tears flowed from his eyes and bathed the Guru's feet. The Guru raised Sajjan's head from his feet with his own hand and said, " There is no cause for despair for God is merciful and reads the heart. You must truly repent and reform your life." " Tell me and I will do what you bid me." "You must recall all the wrongs you have done one by one and then repent from the depth of your heart. Repentance is not a mere repeating of a formula, it is recognition of wrong and driving out tendencies that lead to wrong-doing. The next thing you must do is to find the persons you have wronged and to repay them and seek their forgiveness. The days you spend in redressing wrongs will be the days of your redemption." Then the Guru instructed him in the first stanza of Japji Sahib and how to feel the presence of God in waking and sleeping hours.

Sajjan obeyed and spent weary days in finding his victims, and returning to them what he had robbed them of. He suffered indignities and bodily hurt but remained firm with God's name on his lips and became a true Sikh of the Guru. It is said he was the first to build a Sikh Dharamsala for the spiritual and temporal entertainment of all those who sought its shelter.

15

THE GURU WAS GOING FROM VILLAGE TO VILLAGE enlightening people, bringing comfort to the sick, and hope to the hopeless. One day suddenly he exclaimed : "My friend, Rai Bular, wants me, his journey on this earth is coming to an end. I must see him."

With these words he immediately retraced his steps towards his village home and on arriving there went straight to the house of Rai Bular, while Bala and Mardana visited their own families, and informed the Guru's parents of his return. When Rai Bular saw the Guru coming, he tried to rise from his bed but could not do so. " My spirit is at your feet but my flesh is weak," he murmured slowly.

His devotion touched the heart of the Guru who rushed to him and put his hand on his shoulder and said, " The message of thy spirit has reached my heart : it has brought me to you."

Rai Bular with tears in his eyes prayed that as he could not rise and touch his feet, the Guru should touch his head with his feet so that he might obtain salvation.

The Guru put his hand on the head of Rai Bular who felt as if his soul was finally released from the cycle of birth and death. A strange peace entered his heart and with its coming the breath of life departed.

The Guru's father and mother, when they heard of the arrival of their son, rushed to see him ; his mother with tears of joy took some sweets for him. The Guru after spending the day with Rai Bular went with his parents but he came to Rai Bular every day till he passed away soothed into sleep by the Guru from which there is no awakening. Then without stopping even for a day he resumed his wanderings again consoling his parents that he would see them again when they wanted him.

" You are a strange being," said Mardana when they stopped for rest. " You came from a long distance to see Rai Bular, whom you called your friend and yet when he died, you did not shed even a tear."

" Listen," said the Guru to Mardana, " those in whose heart God dwells they return to their heavenly home. Death is nothing but a gateway to birth. Nothing that lives ever dies, it only changes its form. You see the tree under which you sit ; how its leaves have withered. After a short time it will be covered with fresh leaves. Similarly when a man's body is weary the soul leaves the body to receive newer and fresher garments. So goes on this great play of God from eternity to eternity."

16

THE GURU THEN SLOWLY MADE HIS WAY TO TALWANDI where his uncle Lalu, who was few years younger than his father, also lived. The news that his nephew had arrived reached his ears and he hastened to meet him.

" What has come over you ? " he exclaimed as he saw the Guru seated under a tree, the incarnation of joyful peace. " Why have you deserted your father and mother, your wife and children ? "

The Guru bowed respectfully, rose to receive his uncle and then with a smile that disarmed opposition said, " I have not deserted anyone : in fact, I am dedicating myself to the service of the whole human family."

" How can you serve the whole human family when you have left those dearest to you to be served by others ? " asked his uncle.

" My dear uncle," said the Guru, " they who are bound by the chains of attachment delude themselves that they are serving others. They serve their own self-interest. It is only those who have broken the chains that can render service without any desire for fruit."

" It is good to serve one's parents," said Lalu.

" Yes," said the Guru, " but remember we can receive a richer inheritance if we feel, as I feel, and enter a larger and happier family, such as I have entered. Hear now

" Forgiveness is my mother
Contentment my father
Truth the uncle

These have subdued my mind.
How can other relationships be good
Which holds the human mind in chains ?
Aspiration is my brother
Love for all beings my son
Patience my daughter—
See what a delightful relationship I enjoy.
The result is
That peace is my constant companion
Wisdom my serving maiden
The One Onkar, the creator, my lord and master,
Sayeth Nanak, He who forsaketh Him
And clingeth to others
Courts nothing but misery."

Lalu bowed his head, he could say nothing. After a short stay, the Guru left for Sultanpur. Nanki, his sister, welcomed him to her home. She shed tears of joy at seeing him and made him comfortable, served him with his favourite dish ' kheer' (rice and milk) which he enjoyed.

The Master stayed there for three days. The days he spent in Sultanpur were devoted to the preaching of his doctrine of love. He told all those who gathered round him that love of earthly things was the source of pain and love of God the source of joy. If we could see His hand in pleasure and pain and joyfully accept what came, suffering would lose its sting and joy bring a sense of infinite bliss. He said, " To serve His creation was to serve Him and to make the sacred name the sustenance of life, the way to salvation."

On his way to Kurukhshetra the Master stopped at Sirhind. A godly faqir lived in the town who came to see the Guru. As he approached, the Guru got up and went forward to meet the faqir. They embraced each other and sat down together.

The faqir asked the Guru, "When is a person qualified to put on the garb of a sadhu or faqir ? "

The Master replied, " When he has realised the impermanency of things and the mind is eager to take refuge in the Lord."

The faqir asked, " How is the mind awakened with true desire ? "

The Guru replied, " When the mind becomes aware of the unchanging essence within the changing world."

17

THE GURU WENT FROM VILLAGE TO VILLAGE INSTRUCTING people. He spoke to Hindus and Muslims alike and they listened to him with attention. They gathered round him like bees round a honeycomb. He made no attempt to proselytise, but people received his gospel in all sincerity and enrolled themselves as his disciples. The Guru completed his tour of the villages and cities of the Punjab and then came and stayed at a place on the banks of the Ravi not far from Batala. People flocked to him, Hindus, Muslims, sadhus and faqirs and depressed classes. They heard in the morning the hymns that were sweetly sung and then the Guru gave them instructions.

The good news spread far and wide that where the Guru dwelt falsehood found no place, truth was proclaimed and only the sacred name of God was expounded.

The Karoria who was a Muslim and the owner of the area waxed wrathfull. He resented an infidel becoming so popular. At last he decided to go and tell the Guru to move away from his land. He mounted his horse and with a goodly following started. He had not gone far when his horse stumbled and he fell headlong on the ground. He suffered no serious injury but his followers brought him back home.

He rested for a couple of days and then again he started to expel the Guru. He had not gone beyond the gate of his house when he felt that he could not see ; his sight was gone. He dismounted and returned home wondering at the strange happening.

" How has this happened ?" he asked his followers.

" Nanak is a holy man," they said, " and you were going with the intention of expelling him, so God did not allow you to proceed."

" I will show him all respect," he said, and mounted his horse again but as he proceeded he lost his sight again.

" What am I to do ?" he asked his followers.

" Sir you must go on foot," said his followers. " Purge your heart of anger and humbly beg his forgiveness before starting."

The Karoria humbly prayed that he might be forgiven and started on foot. Lo, his sight was restored and he reached the place where the Guru had taken his abode.

He saw the Guru seated calmly, surrounded by people. The sweet music that was being played filled him with an indescribable peace.

He fell at the feet of the Guru, who affectionately asked him to take a seat near him. This mere act completely changed the Karoria and awakened in him the desire to serve the Guru. He got up and said, "O true teacher ! I am blessed at the sight of you. I know I am forgiven. Permit me to dedicate all this area to you. You can found a village."

The Guru smiled, and said, " The land is of Kartar (God) and you are blessed for dedicating it to divine service. We shall call the village Kartarpur, the seat of the Kartar."

In a short while the place grew in importance. Dharamsalas and houses were built and the Guru's family moved to the village. It was from this place that the Guru again went twice out on his long journeys.

Kartarpur became the seat of the Guru. Amidst chanting of the hymns morning and evening and discourses by the Guru, the congregation grew larger and larger and the free kitchen fed all who came.

The Guru himself started a small farm, which he cultivated by following the plough himself. The Guru held that the right way to live was by the produce of one's own labour. The Guru produced not only enough for himself and his family but gave the surplus to the free kitchen.

In his own person he set the example of leading a simple householder's life and realising the spirit of true religion, devoted to God and the service of his fellow-men combining simple life with lofty thoughts, free from outer shams and hypocrisies, metaphysical and philosophical pursuits which keep the mind from truth. By his own example he showed that by righteous living, even amidst gaiety and laughter, salvation could be attained.

18

THE GURU THEN PASSED THROUGH LAHORE AND WAS deeply distressed by its narrow and dirty streets and the large number of slaughtered animals, which provided meat for the inhabitants. The unrelieved poverty of the working classes and ostentatious luxury of the rich impressed him so much that he exclaimed, "The city of Lahore seethes with poisonous oppression."

He left the town ; he could not endure its stifling atmosphere, but could not forget what he had seen, and full of pity for the people he expressed his feelings in a hymn :

Sin occupies the throne,
With greed the financier
Falsehood the commander
Lust and desire as the judges
Who summon and examine men
And pronounce judgments.
The people in their ignorance
Are without power
They too are eager to usurp
What others have.
Priests have forgotten their craft.
They dance, wear masks
Beat drums and adorn their bodies
They shout aloud, indulge in battle songs, and uphold war
Ignorant Pandits with subtle-reasoning
And tricks of their trade strip men and amass wealth
Even those who perform good acts desire fruit
In a vain hope of obtaining salvation.
The ascetics without true knowledge
Leave their hearths and homes.
Everyone considers himself perfect
But if put to the test, says Nanak, not one could prove true.

The Guru left Lahore and went to Talwandi. On his way he stood outside a village temple watching worshippers offering flowers and tinkling temple bells.

One of the worshippers seeing the Guru standing thoughtfully as an interested spectator accosted him. " What are you looking at," he said, "go in and worship the God inside."

The Guru smiled and said, " Are you not aware of the God within you ? Learn

" Repeat the name of Rama
And thus perform inner worship
Meditate over the word of the True Teacher
He is all-pervading.
How can I worship in temples other gods
When I see the only One and no other ? "

" Do you come every day to worship ? " enquired the Guru.

" No, " he said, " but this is the twelfth day of lunar month and therefore after fasting on the eleventh day *Ekadshi* I worship God to acquire merit. "

" My dear friend, " said the Guru, " under what delusions are you labouring ? You think because you visit the temple and offer a few flowers, you have done a religious duty. The twelfth day would be blessed if you were to give in charity, inspired by a true feeling of compassion, if you were to control the outgoing mind and restrain it within. Fasting from food is a mere penance. We fast truly when we renounce the fruit of our action. We pray truly when we repeat the name of God and hear it repeated from within and thus realise that the One pervades the three worlds. True worship is rendered by knowing the real from the unreal."

The worshipper fell at the feet of the Guru and asked for further instruction.

" My friend, know this truth that God is in every heart and every heart is His temple. It is through His blessings that we can approach Him, then the heart loses its hardness and it is filled with His love. By meditation the sense of duality is lost and Jiva Atman becomes one with the Supreme Atman. By the favour of the Guru, this way is found. The heart is linked with God. Time no more rings down that curtain that we call death. "

19

THE GURU SLOWLY TRAVELLED FROM VILLAGE TO VILLAGE and reached Pakpattan and rested under a tree outside the town. Mardana tuned the Rubab and began to sing

Thou Thyself are the writing tablet
Thou the pen and thou the writer
Thou art also the written word
Thou art the One, there is no other.

There lived at Pakpatan a great saint, Behram. He was called the second Farid and was the head of a school of Sufis. A disciple of the Sheikh, who came to collect fuel for his master's kitchen, heard the hymn, and was deeply moved by its spirit. He came and sat near the Guru.

He was so impressed that, on his return, he reported to his master that there was a saint sitting under a tree with his two disciples. The strange part of it was that he looked like a Hindu while he who played the Rubab looked like a Muslim and sang of the oneness of God.

The Sheikh was interested and told his disciple, " Go and ask him a question : There is one God but there are two ways ; which should we accept and which reject ? "

The disciple returned, bowed respectfully, and repeated the question. The Guru smiled and said, " There is only one God and there is only one way, stick to the one and reject the other. "

Sheikh Behram was greatly struck by the directness of the answer and decided to go and see the Guru himself. He came and greeted the Guru with Assalam-o-Alaikum. The Guru answered, " I salute the indescribeable. "

" Your reply is mysterious, " said the Sheikh. " The Hindus deny the God of Islam and Muslims accuse the Hindus of worshipping many gods. Yet you say, there is only one God and the one way. "

" There is no mystery about it, " answered the Guru. " The ignorant impose their own darkness on the light of truth. They who see divisions do not know God. Those who know Him proclaim His unity.

God is one
He is not subject to change
His light is the life of creation.
That which is born and dies
Cannot be the object of worship
Worship the one God,
Who pervades earth and water.

The Sheikh was very pleased. " I am indeed blessed at the sight of you. I feel

I could discard my robes
And wrap myself in a rough blanket
Or wear that which would
Bring me near to my Lord."

The Guru smiled sweetly and said :

" Why discard clothes
And wrap thyself in blanket
If thy heart is pure and thy devotion intense
God himself will grace thy home. "

" My dear Sheikh, " he continued, " know the truth ; these outer forms are of no account ; it is the inner grace that counts. It is not necessary to dress as a mendicant or to leave home. The one thing needful is to remove the impurities of the mind, and fill the heart with longing to receive His grace. Just as the true desire of a maid, her faith and devotion draws the beloved to her, so does a devotee draw the Lord by his true-hearted consecration to His service. The power of a growing love is great. Remember the spark of true love is never lit in the heart till it is empty of self and filled with faith, fidelity and devotion. God himself cannot resist the love of a devotee. He manifests himself to his devotee and then the devotee is aware only of the beloved."

The Sheikh was moved to the core. "The man who fails to realise God is like the maid," he said, "whose desire is unquenched and who even in her grave cries for her heart's desire, for union."

"The Supreme Lord cares little for looks, dress or appearance," said the Guru. "A contrite heart, a pure life, kindled with true devotion wins His approval. If I were asked, how I would adorn myself to meet the Lord, my answer would be with sweetness of speech and cultivation of virtue. In these attired richly, I would allure the Lord. Humility in action, forgiveness in conduct and words that are like balm are true adornments of the soul. They win approbation in the divine presence for all times. They who are of humble behaviour, without any pride of self, forbearing and helpful, overlooking the faults of others, harmless in action and speech are on the path of achievement."

The Sheikh exclaimed, "You are a true teacher, you are of God and God is in you. May I ask you another question ?"

"What need is there for a question ?" answered the Guru, "The devotees of God think and speak nothing else but of God. As beauty of form attracts the passionate, food the hungry, wealth the greedy, bed the weary and abuses the angry, so does a devotee dwell in silence on God. We must remember that this earth is not an abiding place for us. In eating, drinking, laughing and sleeping we forget death. Selfish desires and bodily comforts rob us of our power to seek the feet of the Lord. We must remember that life here is transitory. We must prepare for the other side."

"It is easy to speak of God," said the Sheikh. "It is not so easy to kindle the heart with true devotion." "Listen !" said the Guru.

Sheikh Farid has said :

"They indeed are true-hearted
In whose heart dwells nothing but love of God.
They who have one thing in their hearts
Another on their lips
Are immature and unripe ;
They forget Him
And only burden this weary earth.
They are truly imbued with the Divine
Who stand straight in His sight
Like beggars at His gate
With love of the Lord in their hearts.
Blessed is the mother
Who begot them
Blessed the earth
For they are its ripe fruit.
The Lord is timeless and unknowable
He is all-forgiving.
Those who know this truth

Like Farid, receive the gift of love as alms.
I kiss their feet
Take refuge in them."

The Guru and the Sheikh enjoyed each other's company and the Guru stayed with him. Many received the instruction from the Guru during his stay. A few years after the Guru again paid a visit to the Sheikh.

20

FROM PAKPATTAN, THE GURU MOVED ON TO MULTAN. THE city was known as the abode of Sufis, God-intoxicated Faqirs. The Guru sat near the mausoleum of Pir Baha-ud-Din, which was then in the charge of a celebrated Sufi who was acknowledged as Pir.

The news that a wandering *sant* had taken his seat in the neighbourhood of the mausoleum reached him and he sent one of his disciples with a cup brimful with milk to the Guru.

The messenger came and without a word presented the cup to the Guru. The Guru smiled, picked up a jasmine flower and placed it on the cup full of milk and told the messenger to take it back to his master.

Mardana was mystified and enquired, " what is the meaning of all this ? "

" The Pir," said the Guru, " meant that Multan was as full of saints as the cup of milk and there was no room for another. I told him that I would be like the jasmine flower that floats on the overflowing cup."

The symbolical answer pleased the Pir, who came to meet the Guru with some of his disciples. The Guru got up to receive him and after greeting each other they sat down.

" From where have you come ? " enquired the Pir, " and what is your religion ? "

" I have come from where we all come ; from Him who is the source of all existence. I belong to His religion."

" Do you believe all is that or all is from Him ? " enquired the Pir with a twinkle in his eye.

The Guru looked straight into his eyes and said, " Only he, who has seen Him, can say with confidence that He is all and everything comes from Him."

" I would not have asked you," answered the Pir. " unless I was sure that you are in communion with Him. There is a halo round your head, which is light itself."

" Know this," said the Guru, " that those who realise Him, for them there exists nothing but God, but as long as the sense of self remains, the sense of separateness of the world from the reality does not disappear."

" Tell me how this world came into being," enquired the Pir.

" Need you know this ? " answered the Guru. " Is it not more important to destroy the sense of separateness in which the world has existence and attain union with God. It is only then you can find an answer to why and how."

The Pir was moved to the core and rose to kiss the hands of the Guru.

The Guru went into an ecstasy at this act of brotherly love and asked Mardana to play on the Rubab as he sang the following hymns :

Come, sister, let us embrace each other
We belong to the one.
Now that we have come together
We shall talk of our beloved Lord :
His are all virtues
All evils are in us.

All things exist
Because of Him
Meditate on the one word
His divine name.
Be absorbed in it
Lose all sense of separation.
And become one with Him.

" Listen my friends," said the Guru, " it is through the sacred word that we rise from consciousness of self to universal consciousness and in that union we see only Him. Great are His powers, greater indeed are his gifts. All living beings, big and small, praise Him day and night. It is in the company of true seekers, the righteous, endowed with virtue, that the true path is discovered ; fear and hate which agitate the mind are destroyed and, out of limitless compassion, the true Lord raises the weak human being and makes him His own. The only way to find the path is to approach the perfect devotees who have become His. We need only know how and in what virtuous ways they realised Him. They will tell you that they adorned themselves with the virtue of self-surrender and its fruit, contentment, peace and sweet speech. For a true devotee, there exists nothing but God, but to become a devotee, perfect purification is required. It is only then that a devotee can dedicate himself to God."

The Pir sent away his disciples and then asked, " You have spoken of the name, the sacred word. What power is inherent in the name of God ? "

" The word," replied the Guru. " is the first manifestation of the unmanifest, from it flowed the whole universe, and it has, therefore, the power to draw unto itself that which flowed from it. The name is the only representation of the creator. It can be uttered in truth in all its power after complete purification of the mind and the heart. The embodied Jiva Atman can become one with the formless, by discarding the attributes which imprison it."

The Pir asked, " Can you prove the power of the word to reabsorb and recreate ? "

The Guru smiled and said, " Calm yourself," and with these words he put his hand on the head of the Pir and uttered the divine word, and in an instant the Pir was reduced to ashes and then again the Guru looked at the ashes and uttered the word and the Pir appeared sitting in his place, saying La-Ilaha-Il-Lilla.

The Pir fell at the feet of the Guru and begged him to teach him the way to salvation. The Guru gave him his blessings. After a few days the Guru decided to move on, but the Pir requested him to stay. The Guru answered him in a hymn :

It would be right to make a permanent abode
And escape the pain of daily wandering,
If there were a permanent place
And this word were unchanging.

What kind of place is this world ?
Impermanent and transitory.
It is wise to cling to the light of the name
And keep ready for the journey.

Yogis perform postures.
The Mullas dwell in holy places.
The Pandits expound sacred books.
The Sidhs occupy the abode of the gods.

Demi-gods, Sidhs, Pirs and Sheikhs,
Heavenly Musicians and Munis
Saints, sages and commanders
Have all to depart.

Emperors, kings, princes and nobles
Have all to march away.
Man has no abiding place on earth
Understand O man ! thou too must go.

This truth has been repeatedly revealed
Yet few pay heed to the truth.
Nanak humbly asserts
The permanent pervades on earth and waters.

The Allah, the unseen, the inscrutable
The omnipotent, the creator, the merciful,
Is alone permanent :
The whole world is in a state of flux.

He alone is permanent
Who is freed from the bondage of cause and effect ;
The heavens and earth shall pass :
He the compassionate one is permanent.

The sun travelleth by day
The moon by night
Hundreds and thousands of stars are moving
He alone is permanent, says Nanak

With these words the Guru bade an affectionate farewell to the Pir and resumed his journey.

21

THE GURU ON HIS WAY BACK STOPPED AT A PLACE CALLED Mian Mithe ka Kotla near Pasrur, and sat in a grove of fruit trees. Mian Mitha, a well-known holy man, lived there.

He heard that a Darwesh Nanak had come. Mian Mitha came out to see the Master. On arriving there he saluted the Guru to which the Master responded and asked Mitha to sit beside him. Mian Mitha then said: " First the name of God, second the name of the prophet. If you recite His Kalma, you will be accepted."

" Yes," said the Guru, " the name of God if uttered by a pure heart and pure tongue can redeem even the sinner. But they who deal in falsehood will reap the reward of falsehood."

A crowd gathered round them to hear their discourse as Mian Mitha had a great reputation as a man of God and a great Sufi Faqir.

" Tell me, you who seem so wise," asked Mian Mitha, " whom does God like ? "

The Guru said, " In His court, high and low, rich and poor, are all alike. He who is true to the core and humble in his behaviour gains the favour of the most high."

" What about the great ones of the world?" enquired Mian Mitha.

" They are like an elephant," the Guru said, " who feeds on butter and sweets trumpets in its pride of strength and throws dust over its head, and lies in dust when death overtakes it. Good men are like birds, fluttering in the air, full of joy, content with the little that meets their needs and which God provides. An egoist enjoying sense objects may excite attention but the barb of the ego gives him no peace. His suffering is equal to his wrongful living. It is the humble and the meek with few needs who remember God and they are blessed."

" You are right," admitted Main Mitha, " but what is the origin of suffering ? "

" The root of suffering is evil—the greed of self which burns like an unquenched fire, the more it is fed the stronger its flames rise. They say this world is a place of suffering, dominated by desire. They cannot give it up and so the root of suffering remains and men like flies die in search of the sweets of life. They who by God's grace overcome desire cross the troubled sea of suffering."

" Tell me," asked Mian Mitha, " how does a person become fit to enter the Court of God ? "

" The glamour of illusion cannot be penetrated," said the Guru, " nor can any weapon cleave it. The only way to escape from it is to submit to the will of God. Then the greedy mind turns back from the objects of desire. "

" How can this be attained ? " asked Mian Mitha

" Act on what the books teach," said the Guru.

" How can a lamp be lighted without oil ? "

" Make fear of the Lord the wick and light it up with discrimination between the real and the unreal. The lamp will burn without oil and in its light the Lord Himself will be seen."

" How can one present a clear account at the end of life ? "

" This world is a place of coming and going and when thy account is called up, release would be the reward of true service. Therefore, serve His creation with all thy might to gain admission to His presence unload the burden of actions, which form the cause and create Karma."

" What you say is true," said Mian Mitha. "I feel as if I have not been acting on what the Holy Book teaches. I have not dedicated my life to service of God and His creation, but now tell me the hidden power of the sacred man."

" Close your eyes," said the Guru, who said 'La' ; as he uttered the word the whole creation disappeared and then he uttered 'Allah, and the creation came into existence again.

Mian Mitha opened his eyes bewildered by the power of the word.

" Know," said the Guru, " that the word brought the universe into existence and the word can gather it back again."

Mian Mitha then humbly asked, " Give me a code of instruction and right behaviour." The Guru said :

" Conceit is the ruin of the soul
Lawlessness has its roots in anger.
Lustfulness is satanic
Self-satisfaction undermines faith
Slander darkens the mind
A man without faith is unclean
Greed leads to thieving
Adultery to impurity
Power breeds tyranny, justice purity
Honesty adds lustre to the face
Dishonesty robs it of refulgence
Honesty befriends, dishonesty betrays
The sword is for warriors
Justice for kings.
The tender-hearted are pure
They who have knowledge are humble
The uncovetous are lifted high
The praise of God washes the mind clean
Contentment marks a faqir
Its absence marks a hypocrite
Faith is the true friend
The characteristic of an infidel is faithlessness
Follow the way of spiritual advisers
It is the right way
The other is without spiritual guidance.
They who seek the presence of God are favoured,

Others do not court his favour.
He is a wise man says Nanak
Who knows these truths
And makes them known to others.''

After giving these instructions to Mian Mitha the Guru left the place.

22

THE GURU PROCEEDED TO A NEIGHBOURING TOWN WHERE a fair was taking place in honour of a faqir, who called himself ' Sada Suhagon,' the Eternal Bride. It was said that this was the day when he saw his Beloved and people came from long distances to see the faqir. The Guru walked up to the dwelling place of the faqir, a house surrounded by a high-walled enclosure, but was refused admission to the sanctuary. The door-keeper said, " He is in communion with the Beloved."

The Guru laughed and said, " I must lift the curtain."

" What do you mean ? " said the crowd which gathered round him.

" Go and see," said the Guru, " who he is in communion with."

The crowd received his word as a command, which it could not disobey and pushed passed the door-keeper and entered the sanctuary. They found the faqir flirting with women, who had come to worship him and had been specially admitted.

The Guru in the meanwhile retired to a mango grove close by. He was sitting full of joy, when a crippled beggar came dragging himself to touch his feet. The Guru looked at the cripple with an eye full of compassion. He uttered *Sat Nam* and sprinkled some water on the cripple, and in an instance the cripple dropped his crutches and walked as if he has never suffered from any infirmity. The cripple walked back to the town and the news spread all over the place.

On the other side the faqir ' Sada Suhagan ' was being pursued by the crowd. The crowd had dismantled his banners and drums and broken his doors. In despair he ran to the Guru to take his protection, and fell at the Guru's feet saying, " Save me and instruct me. "

The crowd fell back at the Guru's command.

" Sit down," he said to the faqir, " you have been unveiled, but with no other purpose than that you may leave the wrong way and take the right one."

" How can I do it, O teacher ? " asked the faqir.

" You must no more deceive people, make your heart pure and see Him, not in any particular form but in all that exists. The Beloved resides in you and in all that there is. It is not by wearing bridal garments that the bride-groom is won. You who claim to be the bride of Him who never dies, you must know that you cannot deceive the All-Seeing, who knows our inner-most thought. It is by following truth that you can gain honour. Even the world applauds those who follow the right path."

" Bless my house with your presence," pleaded Sada Suhagan, " and teach me the way."

" Will you promise to give up this false show and do as I tell you ? "

" I will obey you, my master," he answered.

The Guru then walked to his house and took his seat in the audience chamber which was now crowded with eager pilgrims.

" Listen," said the Guru :

" Foolish one, why art thou self-satisfied ?
Why does thou not enjoy the Beloved in thine own house ?
The beloved is within you, why seekest thou him outside.
Adorn thy eyes with the antimony of His fear
And imbue thyself with the adornment of love.
If He looks at thee with favour
Then indeed would thou become a bride."

" How can I win His love ? " asked Sada Suhagan. " How can I become acceptable ? "

" You ask me," said the Guru, " what is a young and ignorant person to do, if she fails to win His love, in spite of all her efforts, her grief and her tears ? I must tell you, howsoever one may try, without right action nothing is gained. How can she win her Lord when the darkness of desire and greed and the delusion of Maya possess her mind. As long as they hold sway, the beloved cannot be found."

" Then how can He be found ? " asked Sada Suhagan.

" Get rid of these aforementioned enemies and then go and ask those who have won His favour," said the Guru, " by what means they have won the Beloved ? They will tell you. Learn to abide by His will and accept what comes with gladness, wisely carrying out His command. He whose love is everlasting, fix your mind on His feet. Whatever He says must be obeyed, and mind and body consecrated to His service. It is thus, say they who have attained, that the Beloved can be found."

" Tell me more about it," said Sada Suhagan. " My mind is slowly becoming clear."

" Listen," said the Guru. " It is by losing the self that God is found, no cleverness is of any avail. The day He looks at thee with favour, only that day counts, for it is then that all the longings of the soul are fulfilled. She who is loved by her bridegroom is indeed blessed. She is exalted, imbued with the love of her Lord, absorbed in His love, day and night ; such a one is beautiful beyond compare, is indeed truly wise."

" What is love ?" asked Sada Suhagan. " Some people call passion love."

" Love," said the Guru, " cannot be defined in words. It can only be experienced. It is an act of complete self-surrender, an act of inner consecration, which is beyond human power to control. When we love God, we find Him in the temple of our heart and in the heart of all that lives and thus, in loving Him, we love all that exists."

The crowd sat spell-bound listening to the Guru's instructions and experiencing a surge of true emotion.

The Guru then recited a hymn :

" This body is filled with delusion
Desire is its ruling passion
How can it find favour with the Lord ?
The bride robed in false garments cannot attract her bridegroom.
Imbue thy garment with true-hearted devotion
Its colour cannot fade and it can never be seen
They who have dyed their garments in the colour of devotion
They are always with the loved one.
The dust of their feet, says Nanak
Is all that we need seek.
I am sacrifice to those who utter His name,
On them He Himself bestows His glance.
Nanak when the bride is so adorned
He accepts her Himself."

23

AT KARTARPUR SEEKERS OF TRUTH CAME FROM LONG distances as moths gather round a light and asked questions and received instruction.

" We are told by you to remember God and to serve Him," asked a Sikh. " How can we do so ? We repeat the word but only our lips move. Our hearts are not freed from self-seeking propensities."

" It is only through His favour that power to remember Him is gained. Then the heart becomes soft," said the Guru, " selfish motives die within us, the lower self becomes one with the higher self. By the kindness of the Guru, the clue is obtained and the mind is linked with God. Death does not destroy Him."

" The path is dark and dreary," said the Sikh, " until it is illuminated by Divine Light."

" Yes," said the Guru ; " but listen : "

" When the mind dwells constantly on the True One
It is illumined by His light,
And becomes detached from the poisons of the world.
Such is the greatness of the Guru
That salvation is obtained in the midst of wife and children.
If the devotee serves in this way,
That he surrenders his self
To Him whom it belongs
The Lord accepts his surrender.
Such a devotee is exalted,"

All the Sikhs bowed and besought the Guru to continue instructing them :

"Establish in your heart the image of the Guru,
You will gain what you desire.
The Lord favours such a devout servant—
Such a servant has no fear of death.

" Agaln," said the Guru :

" He should discriminate
Between the real and unreal,
He should love the voice of truth.
Such a one attains salvation.
In the practice of word are
Contained all recitations and austerities."

The Guru then went to the river bank and sat watching the fisherman and then he turned to his disciples and said :

" This Jiva is like a fish.
Lured by the objects of desire
The thirst for things leads him into a fisherman's net.
The blind man does not see
And walks into the noose of death
Says Nanak. The mind is not aware,
Is enslaved by its own propensities.
The Lord saves him whom He favours."

24

THE GURU AFTER A FAIRLY LONG SOJOURN AT KAPURTHALA started for Mecca and joined a party of faqirs. The Guru wore a long yellow robe on which were impressed some words and carried a staff such as a Haji carried.

The faqirs watched him and one day asked, " What is your religion ? "

" I belong to the religion of those who follow the path of God," replied the Guru.

The faqirs pressed him to confess that he was a Muslim but the Guru refused ro do so. The faqirs were greatly troubled. They were not sure whether they were right in having with them a man who was an infidel. The Guru read their hearts and disappeared from amongst them with his two attendants. They noticed that a cloud that used to protect them from the scorching rays of the sun also disappeared with him.

The faqirs thought that travelling by himself he would never reach Mecca. They were astonished when they found that the Guru had already arrived with his two attendants. They were even more puzzled when they were told that the Guru had been there for several days. They were convinced that he was some great soul and begged him to forgive them for their suspicions about him.

The keeper of the Kaaba one night discovered that he was sleeping with his feet towards the Kaabo. It was time for prayers so he informed the priest that a pilgrim was committing a great sacrilege by turning his feet towards the house of God. The priest in high dudgeon rushed to where the Guru was sleeping.

" Wake up, you stupid fool," he exclaimed, " and rub your face on the ground and beg to be forgiven for turning your feet towards the house of God."

The Guru did not move, but said, " Turn my feet towards the place where God does not dwell."

The priest could no more control himself and ordered the keeper to take him by the feet and turn him right about in the other direction. The door keeper obeyed but whichever direction they turned the Guru's feet they say that the Kaaba turned with them. The priest stood spell-bound. He saw that the house of God was in all directions.

The Guru rose and looked at the priest with eyes full of compassion, " Your eyes have been opened just for a moment," he said. " Don't forget what you have seen. The entire space is nothing but God's dwelling place."

The priest bowed before the Guru and then told his Chief of what had happened. The Chief was a seeker after truth. He hastened to the Guru in the hope of getting some glimpses of the eternal light.

He respectfully saluted, the Guru returned the salute, and then he sat down beside him.

" You are a godly man from all appearance," said Rukin-ud-Din, for this was his name, "but tell me to what religion you belong."

" I believe in the religion of Him, who is the master of all that is visible and invisible." answered the Guru.

" What do you mean by Him ?" asked Rukin-ud-Din.

" He who is without a second," said the Guru, " to whom birth and death are not known. Who is beyond all change, and who pervades everywhere, lands, seas, air and skies."

" So you believe in one God ; you must be a Muslim."

" I accept no creed, " said the Guru. " I am His slave and slaves have not even their own will. How can they accept any creed who yield unwavering obedience to the Lord? "

" God as you have described Him, is the same God of which our Kalma speaks, " repeated Rukin-ud-Din. " Why not acknowledge yourself to be a Muslim ? "

" The Vedas too speak of one God, the supreme God of all," said the Guru. " Then why should not I declare myself a Hindu ? Truth remains Truth. It is the coloured lenses of the self that reflect it in various colours. A servant of God, aware of His presence, cannot accept creeds, which imprison truth and impose on it their own limitations. "

" How do you make this out ? " asked Rukin-ud-Din.

" You have an example before your eyes. You call this sacred temple a house of God. If you were a true believer, you would find there is no place where the house of God does not exist. Further, you say you believe in one God. Then why don't you recognise in men of diverse creeds a brother ? If this truth dwelt in your heart, you would act in its light. You would not believe that kissing a black stone was the highest religious act. "

Rukin-ud-Din was much impressed and said, " Come and join us to-morrow in the ceremony of sacrifice. I will provide a camel for you."

The Guru laughed and asked, "Why ? "

" God is pleased with sacrifices, " replied Rukin-ud-Din. " He bestows His mercy on those who offer a sacrifice."

" If a drop of blood pollutes your garments," said the Guru, " how can the spilling of blood be pleasing to God ? "

" I do not know," said Rukin-ud-Din, " but sacrifice is prescribed by Shariat—the sacred law of the Muslims. To follow the law is the best of acts."

" The law of love ordains that one should be harmless in thought and act," said the Guru. " To treat others as you would that they should treat you. Righteousness is the unalterable law of living of all people."

" If you follow no written law, what about giving justice to others ? "

" If we live justly, the need for administering justice does not arise. If we forgive those who harm us, we need invoke no man-made law. If we live as members of one human family, every individual living for the others, then we follow the divine law and if we follow the divine law we transform this world full of misery into a world of happiness. In such a kingdom there is no need of any law and for any administrators of law. It is because we fail to follow the divine law that we submit to man-made law to rectify the self-aggrandisement of men."

" How are sinners to be punished, if we do not follow the Shariat ? " asked Rukin-ud-Din. " Tell me what is your conception of sin ? "

" We sin," said the Guru, " when we fail to follow the divine law of love. We sin when we trespass on the rights of others for our own selfish ends, when we cause them injury. In short, to do harm is to sin."

" Such acts as do no harm to anyone and yet have their root in self, are they not sinful ? "

" God reads hearts. He sees what passes in our minds ; unselfish acts partake of the spirit of sacrifice and such acts are blessed, while selfish acts bring pain and suffering."

" What do you mean by sacrifice ? " asked Rukin-ud-Din. " You refused to sacrifice when I invited you to do so."

" My good friend, we sacrifice when we deprive the self of what it holds dear, to serve others or to serve a good cause. To kill a sheep and feast on its flesh is no sacrifice," answered the Guru. "To give what one needs for one's self to another, whose need is greater, is an act of sacrifice. They who give and expect a return make no sacrifice. They are like a money-lender who makes advances at compound interest. They who give and want nothing in return are the real giver, but he who takes all he can without giving is below the human stage. The dead body of an animal and its bones are of some use, but the dead body of a man requires a plot of earth to be buried in or fuel for cremation. He who gives in the hope of a return is human, he who gives without any wish for a reward is divine."

Those who heard the Guru always wanted to hear more from him. The high priest was no exception. He asked, " Instruct me in the art of true living."

" Let your heart and mind put on the garb of a Qalandar. Every hour of the night and day seek your Maker. Rub out from the tablet of the mind all that is written there and polish it into the brightness of a mirror. There will then appear on it a luminous spark. This spark will become the sun and a soundless sound will fill your heart with divine music and draw you near to God.

25

FROM MECCA THE GURU PROCEEDED TO MEDINA AND FROM Medina to Baghdad. He reached there about nightfall and stopped outside the town. It happened to be a place where lepers were segregated and no provision was made for their comfort or treatment.

They crowded round the Guru and made loud lamentations. The Guru was moved and asked them one by one to pass before him. He took some water and sprinkled it on the leper who came before him and he walked away entirely cured. The lepers that were healed next morning ran to the city and spread the news of their healing. The people from the city came in crowds to see the miracle worker and surrounded the Guru.

" Listen, O people," said the Guru, addressing them, " I have worked no miracle. Mercy is of God and He acts through those who are instruments of His will. He is known as Rahim, the Merciful ; He is known as Karim, the Giver, and yet we seek other doors than His."

The Grand Mufti of the city sent a messenger to invite the Guru to his presence.

The Guru said, " I stay where I like ; I go where I like. If the Mufti wishes to see me he can come here."

The Mufti, when he received the message, went himself with all the pomp of his office and sat near the Guru.

" I want to hold discussions with you," he began.

" Discussions are like the wind that blows," said the Guru, " unless there is a spark of fire in the heart which can be blown into the fire of devotion."

" What do you mean ? " asked the Mufti.

" I mean," said the Guru, " that discussion is only fruitful if it lights the hidden fire of devotion."

" Do you know the Kalma ? " asked the Mufti, to change the conservation.

" May I repeat the question ? " said the Guru. " Do you know it ? "

The Mufti laughed with scorn. " I am a Muslim. How can you ask me this foolish question ? "

" I asked the question, because I am sure your tongue recites the Kalma, but it passes over your heart as water over a stone."

" The Kalma is my life-breath," protested the Mufti. " What do you mean ? "

" Did not I say that discussion is mere wind ? " said the Guru. "You may recite the Kalma loudly but it does not reach your heart, which is full of other needs."

" How is that ? " asked the Mufti.

" You begin by saying that there is no other God but Allah, and yet you call men of other religions infidels. They are also of the one God, who has no second. You repeat the Kalma and yet your heart is not moved with forgiveness, nor your hand moved to give. You love other things better than the one God you invoke. My friend, do you not realise that you render lip service to Allah, while you worship other objects. Allah is on your tongue and that which is other than Allah possesses your heart."

They were continuing the discussion when a man came running and fell at the feet of the Guru. " Protect me, O great one," he begged.

" Tell me who is persecuting you," asked the Guru.

He looked at the Mufti and trembled. " I have been condemned to be stoned to death."

" I remember," said the Mufti, " this man has sinned grievously. He has been sentenced to be stoned to death according to that Shariat. He deserves no consideration whatsoever."

" Ah," said the Guru, " remember the Kalma. God is merciful. God is all-forgiving. We act as God would wish us to act, when we show mercy, when we forgive even our enemies. Do those who administer law in their own person break no law ? The laws of the Holy Quran, nay of God himself, pray for forgiveness. God is merciful. He will forgive you. God commands you to show mercy to this man."

The Mufti felt as if he was commanded by God himself. " I obey you, O great one," he said.

The Guru then instructed the Mufti in the art of right living and discovering the right way to find God, and, after a few days' sojourn, the Guru left Baghdad. The Guru was passing through Iran, when he struck a centre of Sufis. They welcomed the Guru and invited him to occupy a seat near their leader, who offered him food and drink of which the Guru and his attendants partook.

" From where have you come ? " asked the senior Sufi. " And what is your destination ? "

" I come from everywhere into here and I must return from here into everywhere."

" Have you brought any news of the Beloved ? "

" Does not the heart breathe His immanence through our lips ?"

" Why is there such ignorance about Him then ? " asked the Sufi.

" As light is located in darkness " answered the Guru.

" Why does the sun set ? " asked the Sufi.

" The sun never sets. It is just a dot that makes day and night."

" Where is light to be found ? " asked the Sufi.

" In the darkness itself," answered the Guru. " The dawn of the morning is hidden in the gloom of the night."

" What is the secret of darkness and light ? " asked the Sufi.

" There is none," said the Guru. " Both are the same. There is darkness in light and light in darkness. To lose the self is to become light ; to assert the self is to become darkness. Self-assertion freezes the self into darkness. The fire of love melts the self into light."

" The blessings of God be on you," said the Sufi. " You indeed are a knower."

26

ON HIS WAY FROM BAGHDAD THE GURU STOPPED IN A village, when a faqir came to the Guru and after an exchange of salutations said, " My Pir has sent me to you to request you to visit him. He is most anxious to meet you."

" How did he know that I was here ? " asked the Guru.

" My Pir is endowed with the light of the spirit," answered the faqir.

The Guru smiled and accompanied the faqir to the abode of his master, who came forward to receive him with a number of his disciples and conducted him to his simple abode.

The Guru stayed with him for a few days. The leader of the Sufis enjoyed the company of the Guru and the communion of the spirit, while his disciples often asked the Guru to solve their difficulties.

One of them one day asked, " Tell me something about the ' Friend ' ? "

" How can I describe Him ? " said the Guru. " How can the tongue speak about Him, who is the speech of the tongue ? "

" Can you explain mystery of darkness and light ? "

" As the dawn of the new day sleeps in the lap of the night, so light abides in darkness and darkness in light. In this way consciousness of self abides in unconsciousness of self, and selfhood in non-self."

" Why has the world been created ? " asked the disciple.

" To experience its futility and to discard it," replied the Guru.

" What is the object of creation ? " enquired the disciple.

" The body is created only to die. It is the garment of the spirit, which must rise out of its imprisoned self into freedom."

" How can this be achieved ? " he was asked again.

" There is no other way," said the Guru, " but to surrender the self to the Beloved and find satisfaction in what he ordains pleasant or unpleasant, or painful."

" How can we find the way of life in the darkness of the world ? "

" Make yourself the instrument of His will and serve His creation. Actions thus performed feed the sacrificial fire and leave no trace behind. In this way the shadows of separation and hate are dispersed, and the gates of love and union flung wide open, and the Lord and His devotee become one."

" If there is no other but Him," asked the Sufi, " what is the meaning of union ? "

" This mystery no words can explain. It is only resolved when God is realised."

" What prevents our realising God ? "

" The shadow of selfhood," said the Guru. " The awareness of the separate self and the desire for things which haunts the separated self."

" How can this shadow be dispersed ? " asked the disciple.

" By invoking his sacred name and purifying the mind and intellect of all impurities."

" What is the sacred name ? "

" People call Him by various names, but the whole Universe manifested itself from the sound of the sacred name. It is the life of all-life."

" By whatever name men call Him, it is Him the one God they remember. Then why is there sueh antagonism between the Hindus and Muslims ? "

" Ignorance is the cause of all religious conflicts ; people talk and yet fail to realise religion."

" What is the cause of ignorance ? "

" You ask questions," said the Guru, " as if words can dispel the darkness of the mind. Ignorance has its roots in the ego, it does not see Him in all things, but makes Him an image of itself. God alone is true, He is unchanging, all else is untrue. He is beyond life and death, fear, attachment and hate. His name is true."

The disciple was greatly impressed, kissed the hands of the Guru and said, " You are indeed a messenger of God. The light of God is in all that you utter."

THE GURU VISITED DAYALPUR AND STAYED WITH A POOR peasant who was his disciple. He had not been there long, when he was disturbed by the sound of loud lamentations that came from a neighbouring house. The heart-rending cries of a mother touched his heart and he enquired from his host, " What has happened with your neighbour who is so grief-stricken ? "

" She is a poor woman," said his host. " Her only son, on whom she depended for her daily bread, came under the wheel of a bullock cart and broke his leg. He has been in great pain ever since and unable to work."

The Guru was moved with pity, got up and walked to the adjoining hut.

The old woman seeing the Guru entering rose up and fell at his feet: " Maharaj, save my son, save me. We have been sustaining life by dissolving ashes in water and drinking the mixture. No one has come to our help. My son, the prop of my old age, see, he is huddled up with a broken leg and fever that never leaves him." She broke into lamentations again.

The Guru who was compassion incarnate approached the sick man and looked at him with eyes which seemed to carry the nectar of healing. The Guru took a little water, uttered Sat Nam and sprinkled the water on him and commanded, " You are healed, rise."

The man threw off his rags nervously, straightened himself and then stood up. He could hardly believe that he was healed.

The mother was overjoyed to see her son completely recovered. She passed her hand over his broken leg and then she clasped the feet of the Guru full of deep gratitude. " You have saved my life, you have saved my son."

" God is all-merciful," said the Guru, " and His grace is always with those who in full faith seek it and turn to Him for protection."

The Guru turned to the young man and asked, " How do you earn your living ? "

" I am a fisherman," replied the young man. " I catch fish and then sell it in the bazzar and with the money that I get I purchase our daily needs. I earn just enough to keep body and soul together and to serve the meagre needs of my mother."

The Guru said, " This Jiva is like a fish, led into the net of the fisherman (death) by desire. The mind, unconscious of truth, falls into the whirlpool of unending cares, and the mind urged by hunger does not realise the danger and walks into the net. He himself shows the way of union, whom he accepts."

The well-to-do neighbour of the fisherman walked in and asked, " What should a man do to obtain salvation ?"

"My brother, one must love all beings, but to reach that stage one has to make a beginning. If you cannot love your neighbour, how can you love those who are strangers ? When your neighbour was in pain, how could you eat bread quietly and sleep comfortably ? "

In the meanwhile news of the miracle spread over the village and the whole village came to the feet of the Guru and received his blessings.

28

THE GURU MOVED FROM DAYALPUR TO ANOTHER VILLAGE and a Muslim peasant, seeing him, left his plough and invited him to rest a while near his well under the shade of trees and offered to bring him some food from his house.

The Guru accepted his invitation and came and sat near the well. The peasant then asked him, " Tell me, how can one find the way to paradise ? "

The Guru was pleased. " Listen," he said : " Plough your land with right action, sow it with the seed of sacred word, water it with the stream of truth, thus be a good husbandman, and grow faith, without worrying about heaven and hell. Do not waste your life in the intoxication of wealth and the joy of physical beauty. Indulgence in argument is not the way of attainment. In the morass of the body, the mind like a frog is not aware of the lotus. The bee hovering over the lotus reveals the secret, but no one heeds until instructed, over the uninstructed mind the true word passes like the wind without moving it."

A rich banker of the village stopped to rest under the shade of the tree. He asked, " How can this poor peasant understand ? You speak to me and I will answer."

" The simple peasant is nearer God than you," said the Guru. " You are engrossed in wordly desire and deluded by Maya. They are favoured whose heart is kindled with His love, who rejoice in the divine dispensation. Even though you offer prayers five times a day and fast for thirty days, beware lest your actions are actuated by Satan. Remember that you must tread the path of death and all your accumulated wealth will not go with you."

29

THE GURU PAID A VISIT TO SAYEADPUR, AT PRESENT KNOWN as Eminabad, to protect his devotee, Lalo. The town was inhabited by Pathans, who were leading a luxurious life and caring little for others. The Guru asked Lalo to come out of the town as it was threatened. Lalo obeyed and they returned to a grove outside the town.

" What is going to happen ? " asked Lalo.

" As the word of the Lord cometh to me so I make it known.

O Lalo, Babar has hastened from Kabul with a bridal procession of sin and demandeth wealth as his bride.

The call of duty and religion are forgotten ; falsehood marcheth in the van, O Lalo.

Qazis and Brahmins are no more called ; the devil readeth the marriage service, O Lalo.

Mussulman women, followers of the Book, shall in suffering call upon God for mercy.

Hindu women whether of high or of low caste shall meet the same fate;

I hear the paeans of murder and see men smeared with the saffron of blood.

Sing the praises of the Lord in the city of corpses and dwell on this truth.

He who made men, assigned them different positions ; sitteth apart alone and regardeth them.

True is the Lord, true is His decision, true the justice He meteth out.

Bodies shall be cut like shreds of cloth ; Hindustan will remember what I say.

They shall come in 78 depart in 97 and then shall arise a disciple of the Guru,

Nanak uttereth the word of the True One and proclaims the Truth at the appointed time."

They who sat round the Guru thought the Guru was annoyed and was cursing the city. A Braḥmin came forward with offerings of flowers and fruits and begged the Guru to ṛemove his curse from the town.

The Guru smiled and said, " How can I curse His creation ? I am giving you a warning ; remove yourself from the town to a distance of at least twelve miles if you wish to escape the calamity that is threatening the town."

Many people took the warning.

Next day, all of a sudden, Babar with his army arrived and sacked the town and subjected it to massacre, loot and rape. The Guru with Bala and Mardana did not leave the place. He along with his companions was arrested, and was made to carry the loot along with other prisoners. As they walked they saw the load on the head of the Guru and Bala lifted up a foot above their heads and carried by the air. Mardana was given a horse to lead and the horse followed him of its own free will.

The prisoners were taken to a concentration camp and both men and women were given grinding mills to grind the corn. The Guru was also required to do so. The Guru went into Samadhi and and his grinding mill worked without any visible motive power. People observed the strange phenomenon and carried the news to Babar.

Babar could not believe it and himself came to see the Guru. He stood spell-bound as he saw the mill working. He waited till the Guru opened his eyes and then with folded hands bowed to the Guru and begged to be forgiven. The Guru said :

" Thou ruled over Khurasan
Now thou terrifiest Hindustan.
He has sent you the Mughal as a messenger of death.
Has slaughter and lamentations
Awakened no compassion in thee
The Creator is beyond blame.
The Creator is the supreme Lord.
If a strong man beats a strong man
No feelings of resentment arise,

But if a tiger falleth on a herd of sheep
The shepherd is expected to protect.

A Jewel of a Kingdom,
Was neglected by its rulers
Their death will be mourned by none.
O God ! thou givest power to those who combine,
And taketh it away from those who breed discord :
Such is thy glory.

He who considers himself great,
Enjoys himself to his heart's content,
In the eyes of God, he is no better than a worm,
Nibbling at the corn.
He gains who, while alive, learns to die
And repeats His name."

Babar was greatly moved by the words addressed by the Guru. He expressed regret for indiscriminate slaughter. He begged the Guru to come to his tent with him.

"I cannot leave my fellow prisoners," said the Guru.

"They are released," said Babar.

"Listen, O King," said the Guru, "The people here have suffered for their sins, even you cannot escape the fruit of your acts.

Yon have deprived some of their five prayers, others of their hours of worship ;

The Hindu women could not bathe and put the *tikka* on their forehead or eat without their sacred squares.

They cannot utter the name of Rama or of Khuda.

They have lost their homes ; they wander about enquiring after the safety of their relations.

They are destined to sit and weep in pain.

What pleases God, O Nanak, shall happen. What is man ? "

Babar was greatly affected by the utterance of the Guru and begged him to accompany him to his tent. The Guru agreed and accompanied him. When they were seated, a servant, at a gesture from the King, brought two cups of hemp and the King offered one to the Guru.

The Guru smiled and said, " I take no intoxicants, which cloud the mind, their effect passes off. I have taken the intoxicant of love of my Lord, which fills me for all time."

"Listen O King," said the Guru, "survey the scene. Take a warning from those whom you have defeated. Victory and defeat come from God. Do not forget that he who is victorious today may suffer the fate of the defeated to-morrow if he fails to glorify God. They who ruled here yesterday where are they to-day ?

"Where are those games, those stables and those horses, where are those bugles and clarions ?

Where are those who buckled on their swords and were mighty in battle ? Where are those scarlet uniforms ?

Where are those mirrors that reflected fair faces ? We see them no longer here.

This world is thine, O Lord of the earth.

In one moment, thou establishest and disesatablishest.

Thou distributeth wealth as Thou pleasest ;

Where are those houses and those mansions—those palaces ?

Where are those beautiful seraglios ?

Where are those luxurious couches and those fair ones the sight of whom banished sleep ?

Where is that betel, those betel-sellers and those fair maids ; they have vanished.

For wealth many are ruined ; this wealth hath disgraced many.

It is not amassed without sin, and it accompanieth not the dead.

Him whom the Creator destroyeth, He first depriveth of virtue.

Many priests tried by their miraculous powers to restrain the invader when they heard of his approach.

He burned houses, mansions and palaces ; he cut princes into pieces and rolled them in the dust.

No priest hath wrought a miracle, the Mughal hath not become blind ;

There was a contest between the Mughals and the Pathans, the sword was wielded by both in the battle.

One side aimed and discharged their muskets : the other also handled their weapons.

They whose letter hath been torn in God's court, must die, my brethren.

There were the wives of Hindus, of Turks, of Bhattis, and of Rajputs :

The robes of some were torn from head to foot.

Their dwellings were transformed into cremation grounds :

How did they fare whose husbands came not home to pass the night ?

The Creator acteth and causeth others to act ; to whom shall men complain ?

Misery and happiness are according to His pleasure ; who shall hear our cry ?

The Commander issues His orders as it pleaseth him, says Nanak.

Man obtaineth his allotted share."

Babar remained sunk in thought for a long while and then said, " You believe in one God. My religion also teaches what you teach. Embrace Islam, then, on the day of judgment, the Prophet himself will intercede for you."

" O King," said the Guru, 'at the gate of the Lord many messengers stand waiting. There are hundreds of thousands of Mohammads at His Court. Their number cannot be counted. They are sent at His bidding. He sends prophets into the world and recalls them at His will. I know that only God is pure and perfect. All else is impure and imperfect."

Babar was greatly impressed and asked, "What can I do for you ?"

" Nothing," said the Guru. " It is the one God Who hath commissioned me and I enjoy His gifts. To depend on human being and not on Him is to lose both the worlds. The giver is One, the whole world begs at His door. They who forsake Him and attach themselves to others lose all. He makes emperors and kings. No one is His equal. Hear, Emperor Babar, he who beggeth from thee is a fool."

" O true teacher," said Babar, "I beg of you to give me a boon for you are a representative af God."

" Ask, Mir Babar," the Guru answered.

" Give me the throne of Delhi in perpetuity " asked Babar.

" Nothing in this transitory world is permanent," said the Guru. " But your successors will rule for many generations : at least for seven generations."

" You have bestowed on me the kingdom of the earth. Teach me how to enter heaven."

" Be just and never do that which is unjust," said the Guru. " Never depart from the path of truth. Temper justice with mercy, and forgive others as you wish to be forgiven. Do not covet that which is meant for others ; for God is just. Do not act when you are burning with any of the five fires ; always act for the benefit of others. Do not sow the seed of cruelty. He who is cruel, himself suffers cruelty."

The Guru then took leave of Babar and led Lalo back to his home which had been saved by the grace of the Guru.

30

THE GURU STARTED ON HIS JOURNEY AGAIN AND STOPPED at a spot near Hasan Abdal. The Guru sat below a hillock which was occupied by a Muslim faqir known as Wali Qandhari, as he was said to have come from Qandhar. He was said to possess supernatural powers and had a great following of disciples. He had built for himself a house and a sanctuary in which he said he held communion with God on the side of a natural spring, which fed a well in which he collected the water. There was no water available in its immediate neighbourhood.

Mardana was now feeling very thirsty and the Guru told him to go to the top of the hill and assuage his thirst from the well. Mardana accordingly climbed up and approached the well. He saw the Wali sitting near it. Mardana respectfully bowed.

" Why have you come here ?" enquired the Wali.

" I am a servant of Guru Nanak, who is a holy person," Mardana replied. " He is sitting below the hill. I am thirsty. I asked the Guru to tell me where to get water and he directed me to come to you."

Wali was annoyed to hear another holy man coming to the place and not paying him homage.

" Get out," he said. " If your master is a holy man, why does he not procure water for you instead of sending you to me ? I cannot allow you to take water from my well."

Poor Mardana returned disappointed and related to the Guru what had happened.

" Never mind what the Wali said ; go back and ask for water again with all humility," commanded the Guru.

Mardana was tired and thirsty but he could not disobey his master, so he made another attempt and went up the hill and again begged humbly for water.

The Wali shouted, " Go back, tell thy master to produce water for you to drink."

Mardana came back to the Guru tired and thirsty and almost fainting.

The Guru smiled and said, " Mardana, utter *Sat Nam* and dig a little hole where you are sitting." Mardana did as he was ordered. Immediately water spouted up and began to flow.

The Wali who was still sitting at his well observed that it was getting drained.

Mardana quenched his thirst and sat quietly near his master. The Wali was deeply concerned as his well began to get empty. He got up and saw the water flowing at the feet of the Guru. His rage knew no bounds. There was a big stone lying near him. He rolled it down so that it might fall on the Guru and crush him.

Bala saw the big stone coming down and warned his master. The Guru did not move but in time raised his hand to stop the stone. It stopped dead and received the imprint of Guru's hand (panja) on it. This place is known even to this day as Panja Sahib and the imprint of Guru's hand is still visible on the stone and the pool of crystal water bears witness to this miracle.

The Wali was frightened and humbly came down and bowed before the Guru, who received him and asked him to sit down. The Wali sat down and asked the Guru, " Tell me how did you acquire this power ? "

" Waliji," said the Guru, " power belongs to the All-powerful. Human beings are powerless. It is only when we take shelter in Him that He extends His protecting hand. There is no power higher than truth. That which is false cannot endure ; it must fail in the end.

" Listen, O mind, to true advice.
Thy record will be taken out
And thou will be called to render an account.

They whose account is not clear
Will have to face an urgent demand.
The angel of death will hold them
From that narrow lane there will be no escape :
The false will fail
Only the truth shall prevail."

The Wali was deeply impressed. " The Holy Prophet has said *'Learn to die while living.'* How can this be done ? How can we realise that all is His, and which is the best name of God ? "

" If the self dies, when we are living we follow the way of the Prophet ; it is only with the death of the separating self that we realise all is His. By whatever name we remember Him is the best.

The Wali then asked him to come with him to the Dargah and take his seat in the holy place.

" It is difficult to enter the gate of His house and occupy the holy place. I am happy where I am."

They spent a great deal of time together talking of things of the spirit.

31

FROM HASAN ABDAL, THE GURU WENT TO GORAKH HATRI. It is not far from Peshawar, and in that place there is the temple of Gorakh Nath—the Guru of the Hatha Yogis. The Master sat outside the door of the temple. The Yogis had heard about the spiritual power of Nanak. They were anxious to put him to test and to win him as a disciple.

One of the Yogis—Sidha—came and addressed him thus : "O Nanak, we know you are an Udasi, why do you not join our fold ? Come into the temple. Its doors will be opened unto you."

The Guru answered :

" Show me the door, the inner door
Beyond which He dwells and the way to open it—
It is in search of this door
That I am a wanderer."

" What do you mean ?" asked the Yogi.

" Listen," said the Guru, " If you cannot tell, I will.

" Sorrow is the gate, passion is the door-keeper.
Hope and anxiety are the two parts of the door.
The water of Maya fills the moat of the temple.
Inside he is seated
In a state of truth :
By hundred names He is called
Limitless are His names.

The one God has no equal."

" What are you talking about ?" said the Yogi with impatience.

" One must not utter aloud the truth," said the Guru, " One must keep quiet and surrender to His will. Is this what you teach ? "

" No," said the Yogi, " come and we will teach you the way to acquire knowledge and power."

" As long as there is desire, there is anxiety, and, unless desire dies, the aspirant cannot be one with Him," said the Guru.

" Why do you talk nonsense ?" said the Yogi. " Only Yogis know how to span the ocean of life."

" Do they ?" said the Guru. " There is only one way to cross the ocean of life and that is to let the self die while living."

They were still talking when Machandar Nath—the Sidh Guru—joined them. " Thou art young," he said, " and thou talkest of things thou knowest not. Thou wearest the garb of a renouncer without sectional marks. What section dost thou belong to and who is thy teacher ?"

" The One Onkar is my teacher," said the Guru. " I belong to the section of the Formless."

Machandar Nath laughed. " What vain words," he said. "Come and be my disciple, and I will teach you how to practise Yoga."

" Listen," said the Guru, " and hear the true word :

" Listen, O Manchandar, to Nanak.
He who controls the five senses
And does not waver
He attains the way of Yoga.
Such a disciple gets the light.
He remains absorbed in Him
He not only obtains salvation himself but
For his forbears also."

" You talk very wisely but your words are without knowledge. You do not know the secret of securing power," said Machandar Nath.

" He whose consciousness becomes one with the universal consciousness is, even when performing material acts, never moved from the stability which he has attained :

" Longing for bliss
Full of devotion towards God
Steeped in contentment,
Completely satisfied,
Content with what comes unasked,
Established in the divine self,
One with the object of meditation

And absorbed in the true name
Such a one is a Yogi.

"How does a disciple attain his goal? What are his characteristics? enquired another Yogi.

"I will tell you the truth
The real mark of a disciple is
That amidst a sea of desires
He is desireless.
Such a one undoubtedly is accepted by the Creator,"
the Guru replied.

Machandar Nath was surprised. "Do you mean," he asked, "that he who performs the daily routine of a householder can also be stable-minded?"

"Yes," said the Guru, "if he is free from hope and desire."

"How can he without following the path of asceticism and without serving the teacher?" enquired the Yogi. Said the Guru:

"The link between teacher and disciple is formed
When soundless sound is heard,
It is the use of the prescribed cure
Which secures the tenfold knowledge
Of which all the six Shastras speak."

"Why don't you join the creed of Gorakh Nath who was the greatest of Yogis?" asked another.

"My dear friend," said the Guru, "the disciples of Gorakh Nath blow a horn and practise control of breath and carry a beggar's bowl. This is not enough. Listen to the true way of obtaining union.

"In the divine presence I blow the horn (of devotion).
And listen to the soundless sound
Blending my consciousness with it;
The sound which is all-pervading.
Making faith my begging bowl
I beg for the alms of the Sacred Name."

"This sounds true," said the Yogi, "but it is good to join the Yogis and learn the ways of Yoga."

The Guru continued:

"There are saints in various garbs,
Following various methods and striving,
Meet them. Learn to praise God,
Service is the way of attainment
As salt is not dissolved in butter.
As water fails to wet lotus leaves

So a householder is not soiled by his surroundings,
Such a devotee is beyond the power
Of the angel of death, he is powerless against him.
O Yogi, when God is awakened in the heart—
He who has created this world
He is the True Teacher.
Who out of water and other elements created life
He made the sun and the moon, the two lamps,
He made this earth, the place of birth and death.
We forget Him and run after the other."

"Why do you speak in parables, and why don't you speak in simple words ?" asked the Yogi.

"I indulge in no parables," said the Guru. "The Divine spark is dormant in every heart. We do not realise its presence, but when we blend our limited consciousness with divine consciousness, we attain true Yoga." The words of the Guru touched their hearts. They could not refute the truth of his teaching and departed marvelling at what he had said. The Guru then resumed his journey.

32

THE GURU THEN ENTERED THE BEAUTIFUL VALLEY OF Kashmir. Crowds gathered round him wherever he went and received instruction. He reached Srinagar where a very learned Pandit by the name of Brahm Dass lived. He was said to have acquired supernatural powers and was a devotee of the goddess. The news that a great teacher had arrived reached him and he decided to visit the Guru.

It is said that he made the carpet on which he sat fly into the air, so that he might impress and overawe the Guru by this display of his powers. When he reached the place, he saw that a large crowd was sitting there, but he could not see the Guru. He enquired, "Where is the Guru ?"

"He is sitting just in front of you," they replied.

"Why cannot I see him ?" he said.

"How can we tell ?" they replied. "He is before you."

The Pandit was not only annoyed but felt humiliated as his carpet refused to fly back to his place. He had no option but to walk back deeply hurt.

He sat brooding over the incident, when one of his disciples came to see him.

"You have all deceived me," he said. "There was no Guru present, otherwise why could I not see him ?"

"He was there," asserted the disciple. "It is your pride that darkened your vision."

" If you go on foot without pride of power, you will benefit by the sight of him."

The Pandit next day waited in all humility on the Guru and with folded-hands he fell at his feet. The Guru received him very cordially and asked him to sit beside him.

Then the Pandit asked the Guru, " First of all, please tell me why I could not see you yesterday."

" How could you see me in extreme darkness ? "

" There was no darkness. It was broad daylight."

" Is there any darkness denser than pride ? " said the Guru. " Because you could fly you thought you were almost a superman. Birds and insects fly in the air ; are they of any account ? "

The truth struck home. " Forgive me, O teacher," he exclaimed. " I have read sacred books and acquired superphysical powers. I must confess I have found no peace. Tell me how I can touch the feet of the Lord."

" Knowledge which partakes of the darkness of the self is of little avail," said the Guru.

Brahm Dass again fell at the feet of the Guru and exclaimed, " Guru Maharaj, I was mistaken, save me. My time is short."

He had an idol of Shiva tied with a string round his neck, and he removed it there and then.

The Guru said, " You have worshipped other gods, who perish like men ; you have followed men, of much learning, but you have not grasped the truth that is within you. You have sought Him in things which are a mere reflection of reality : you are lost in the wilderness of knowledge. Words only acquire a meaning when you realise the truth of which they are the smybols."

The Guru sang this hymn while Mardana played on the Rubab :

" Another man's wife, another man's property,
Covetousness, evil desire, search of sense objects,
Bad temper, backbiting, lustfulness and wrath—
He who rids himself of these
Will find in himself the Infinite, the Unknowable.
This hidden nectar only he discovers
Who receives the jewel of the Guru's word and makes it his life breath.
He is not disturbed by pleasure or pain.
Good and evil they are all the same to Him.
In the dawn of true wisdom (*budhi*)
Fed by the light of God's name
In the company of saints, devoted to the Guru,
The Guru, the Giver, bestows the sacred name.
Treasuring it, the disciple is absorbed in Him.
He alone obtains the sacred word
Who earns the grace of the Lord.
This body is the temple of the Lord

In the heart is His light
Sayeth Nanak, let the word of the Guru
Enter the heart and by the grace of God
Effect everlasting union."

The Pandit bowed and said, " I have now learnt the truth, to seek within and not outside, to get rid of the evil passions, to seek the favour of the Lord and remain absorbed in the Guru's word."

The Guru nodded assent.

33

FROM SRINAGAR THE GURU TRAVELLED INTO LOWER TIBET and approached a monastery. The Head Lama came to meet him and welcomed him to his monastic home. He offered the Guru refreshments, made him comfortable and then quietly enquired, " They say there are many creeds prevalent down in the plains and the learned expound many philosophies. What do you say about the creation of this world and the Creator ? "

The Guru said :

" From the soundless Absolute proceeds everything.
He the soundless emanates sound
And from it flows forth air, water, fire, light, and souls.
He, the Absolute, remains unaffected and yet maintains all that lives.
He the Lord of creation rejoices in his own creation.
The Absolute produces Brahma, Vishnu, Shiva
And also time and the four great ages.
He who knows the Absolute as all-pervading
Is a perfect man, and in his company delusion is destroyed."

The Lama heaved a deep sigh. " I have heard before the theory of the Absolute and your definition has cleared it a good deal. Tell me more about it."

" The Absolute produces earth and heaven and without any support maintains these. The three worlds come forth from the Absolute and are permeated with the Maya of the Absolute ; they are its manifestations and are absorbed in it. From the Absolute arise differentiations, the species and all the four forms of speech. They are absorbed in it again. From it also arise the seven regions and the fourteen spheres. They are all its creation, caused by it, and to be absorbed in it. From the Absolute proceed day and night, that measures out pleasure and pain. It is by constant search that we find the way to cross the bounds of time, and become immortal. It is thus that righteous seekers find their heaven.

" From the Absolute are radiated sun and moon. The light of the Absolute pervades the three worlds. The Absolute is limitless and indescribable. The Absolute is *Samadhi* itself. The source of the seven seas is the Absolute and also all knowledge. When the human mind, by the power of the word communicated by the Guru, bathes in the lake of truth, it obtains release from the wheel of birth and death.''

The Lama smiled and said, " So the truth of Lord Buddha still remains and the knowledge remains that all beings are tied to the wheel and suffer agonies till they obtain release by following the eight-fold path."

" Yes,'' said the Guru, " the Absolute manifests itself as God, his incarnations are the Avatars. He makes gods, demi-gods, elemental and celestial music-makers, ordained to perform their various duties. He produces the three basic tendencies. *Tamasic*, *Rajasic* and *Sattavic* : of inertia, energy and pure spirit. These are shadows of His manifestations. The spirit imprisoned in five element sows the seed of acts, good and bad, merit and demerit. One's own deeds make the destiny which is inscribed on the forehead of everyone and brings the harvest of one's own sowing through cycles of births and deaths. By Divine grace, when the true teacher imparts the word, the Turia stage is attained, with it the divine consciousness, and with it the gift of freedom from the domination of Gunas—the basic tendencies."

" This too I have heard," said the Lama, " also the great books of knowledge teach the same truth. I like to hear from you, for your words are like shafts of light, which illumine the darkness of the mind."

" The Sam, Rig, Yajur and Atharva Vedas which Brahma is constantly reciting and to which you have referred are books of knowledge. They and even Maya, with its three attributes—Gunas—come from the Absolute. Limited power of expression comes from the Absolute, so no one can describe the Absolute. What we must learn is the cure of suffering which humanity inherits. Suffering ceases when the word of the teacher enters the heart. Only a rare one reaches this stage and receives the gift of emanicipation, such a one is emancipated for all time. He is perfect. He is exalted.''

" What are the attributes of the true teacher ? " enquired the Lama, who was deeply interested and was trying to test the truth of the Guru's teachings in the light of his knowledge of the gospel of Buddha.

" The true teacher is intoxicated with the love of God. He is one with God. He is unique. He is exalted, wisdom and power are his gifts. When good fortune favours a Guru is met. Mind is no more attached to wordly objects. He destroys delusions.''

" Can a philosopher (*giani*) break the bonds of attachment ? "

" No, it is only the true teacher who awakens the Buddhi, supreme wisdom, and opens the door that leads to the Guru,'' said Nanak. " Then the pure sound of the true word is heard and the true name of the Lord enters the heart and *smadhi* is attained.''

The Lama was very pleased and asked ; " How can we reach the Absolute ? "

" The Absolute is in you," said the Guru. " Its light is in every heart. It is only discovered under the instructions of the true teacher. The Absolute is all that is : all is in one and the one is in all. This secret is revealed by the Guru. This secret is known when you know yourself and realise yourself in all beings. He is exalted who recognises himself in all beings.''

" Tell me what stands in the way of righteousness ?'' asked the Lama. " Where is the mind situated ? How can it become an abode of peace ? Show me the way from the unreal to the real.''

"Five passions rooted in desire possess the mind, and these lead the mind astray. It wanders after objects of desire unaware of the inner peace. The mind is in the body. It is the mirror of the True One. It is obscured by desire, but when it is dissociated from the search of that which is false and transitory it finds peace in the True One. The way from the unreal to the real is discovered by purification of the self, by performance of righteous acts and constant striving for spiritual advancement. He who is not truthful, he whose life is unrighteous, cannot understand the meaning of Mukti or Salvation. He who approaches the Primal Being after self-purification attains with ease the union. He is freed from births and deaths, coming and going. He, the devotee of the Lord, becomes established in the Lord. Nothing else exists for him."

" You said that the Absolute is Infinite. How can a finite being become one with the Infinite ?"

" Just as the tree and its fruit are the same," said the Guru. "They who eat the fruit of the tree of immortality and drink its nectar become one with the Supreme. He who knows the self becomes one with the Supreme Self."

" Why does pain haunt those who work for pleasure ? " asked the Lama.

" Pain is but the reflex of pleasure ; when we seek pleasure, we also court pain. The only way to escape pain is to quench the thirst for pleasure, and remain unaffected by both pleasure and pain. Everyone is eager to secure pleasure ; no one desires pain. The ignorant see not the truth that pain follows pleasure. When pleasure and pain become the same, and these two impostors are defeated, the secret word opens the door of true bliss."

34

THE GURU SPENT A VERY PLEASANT DAY WITH THE LAMA, who said that there was going to be a great gathering of saints and sages and masters of wisdom at Lake Mansarowar. He asked whether the Guru would like to go there.

" It is for Mansarowar," said the Guru, " I am bound."

In due time the Guru accompanied by the Lama left the monastery and travelled to the land of perpetual snows, shining in its purity like a sea of Sehri. He there met the great ascetics, the mahatmas, the renouncers of the world and the saints with supernatural powers.

" How is India faring ? " they asked him.

" Why do you ask me ? " he said. " You know that the dark age is like a knife, which kings handle like butchers ; justice has taken wing and flown away. The darkness of untruth obscures even the light of the moon, which cannot be seen. I am perplexed how to show you the true way in this dreary darkness. Humanity is groaning under the dread domination of the self, and yet falsehood must fail, and truth prevail."

"Hail, hail, Nanak," they said, "His light will prevail." The Guru said, "Hail, hail, to Him, the Lord of all."

The Guru passed into a trance and sang the following hymns:

"He is the True One
There is no other.
He sends forth the Universe
And absorbs it in Himself
As it pleases Him.
He keeps us ;
He cannot be questioned.

He is the Creator of the three *gunas*.
He drives us to action and bondage,
And Himself shows the way of freedom
He Himself is all-wisdom,
He Himself is the knower,
He Himself is ever satisfied.

He is air, water and fire,
He is the sun and the moon,
He is knowledge and meditation,
He is the true teacher.
They are not enmeshed
In the net of time
Who take refuge in the True One.

He is the male, He is the female ;
He is the dice, He is the pawn ;
He is the play, He is the player ;
He is the day, He is the night ;
He is the primal being, beginningless, soundless
Dwelling everywhere, the Lord of the world.
He himself listens ; He himself is the true teacher.

He Himself is the tree
The flower and the fruit.
He Himself the bumble-bee,
He Himself is in land and water,
And He Himself the fish and the ocean.
His forms are indescribable.

He Himself the priceless jewel,
He Himself the connoisseur.
He Himself gives and takes away,
He Himself punishes and forgives.

He Himself is the bow and the arrow.
He Himself the handsome archer.

He Himself is the speaker,
Himself the listener.
He who has planned all things—
The air, the Guru ; water, the father ;
Earth, the mother's womb ;
Day and night the nurses ;
Love the guardian ;
Under these as he directs
The play of the world goes on.

He Himself the fish,
Himself the fisherman ;
He Himself the cow ;
He Himself the cowherd ;
In all beings pervades His light
He directs all.

He Himself is the enjoyer ;
He Himself is the lover .
He Himself is the Yogi,
He Himself is the Lord of all,
Without form, without fear and suffering
Himself the perfect *Samadhi*.

The whole creation is in Him,
All that is visible is subject to change.
He is changeless.
They indeed are true teachers
Who know the secret
And gather the wealth of His name.

The secret of the word
Is the gift of the True Teacher.
He is perfect with all powers.
He is in need of nothing.
He is eternal without trace of desire.
He is pure, and separate from all.

The true Guru the giver of knowledge.
Whatever is seen is in Him.
Nanak begs at His door
For the gifts of the name

They who have tasted

The Nectar of the name
Are intoxicated with it ;
They are freed from birth and death.

To his devotees He givest
Peace and salvation."

The Master stopped for a while and then started the chant again :

" True are Thy regions and true Thy universe.
True Thy worlds and true Thy creation
True Thine acts and all Thy thoughts.
True Thine order and true Thy court.
True Thy command and true The behest.
True Thy favours and true Thy songs.
Hundreds of thousands and millions declare Thee true—
True is all Thy power, true all Thy strength,
True Thy praises, true Thy eulogies.
True Thy might, O True King,
Nanak, true are they who meditate on the True One
That which is born and dies is not true."

They who knew the truth needed no more discussions and explanations. They gloried in the presence of a living teacher and enjoyed his company and then on the appointed day, they all departed. Some to their homes in the perpetual snows, others to their monasteries and secluded dwelling places, while the Guru accompanied by the Lama wended his way through the high Himalayas, back to the plains, to the world of men, to relieve the sorrow and suffering of the world and to show the way of everlasting peace.

35

THE GURU TRAVELLED FROM KAILASH AND MANSAROWAR towards Almora and somewhere in the lap of the glaciers met another party of Sidhas—Yogis—with their Guru Gorakh Nath. They were said to possess great power over nature and knew the secret of prolonging their life and retaining vigour of body and mind.

They received the Guru with courtesy and invited him to stay with them.

" Why don't you join us ?" said one of the Yogis. " We will show you how to live through the ages and never grow old. We will teach you to become a true Yogi."

" Can you tell me nothing better than to prolong the agony and to live long years ? I thought a Yogi sought freedom from bondage and was one with God. Know that Yoga is a spiritual union and such union can be effected by abiding by His will and remaining unaffected by the impurities of the world : it is good to be in the world and not to be soiled by the evils of the world. You will admit," the Guru continued, " that the object of Yoga is union." This union cannot be effected by the wandering in the forests or by physical austerities but by submerging the individualised ego in its divine source.

" You," said one of the Yogis, " profess to be a teacher of religion, yet you wear neither the garb of a saint nor that of a Yogi ; to what denomination do you belong ? "

" My name is Nanak," said the Guru, " and I belong to the denomination of God. Listen :

" In every heart He dwells
Dedicate thy will to His service,
Coming and departing is the law,
Accept the divine will.
The true teacher imparts the secret,
Of finding an abiding place in God.
They who follow the word of the Guru
Realise the self and become one with Him."

" You are a contradiction in your own person," said a Yogi. " A householder must act and act for the self and thus make Karma, which must bring him back to earth to go through the cycle of birth and death. How can anyone without renouncing the world destroy the seed of action ? Without its destruction, there is no freedom."

" There is a great distinction between an assertive action and performance of an act without desire for its fruit," said the Guru. " The former binds, the latter frees. He whose mind is charged with the Divine Presence, he is in perpetual solitude in this world of desire ; his thirst for things has been quenched. He who has realised the Unknowable and enabled others to realise Him, he commands respect. He is like a lotus that rises to the surface of a lake or like a swan that floats over the water and is untouched by water. So does a Yogi remain unaffected by his surroundings."

" Please do not be annoyed," said the Yogi. " Pay heed to our request and give a proper answer for we only seek elucidation. We want to know if you have found a better way than ours."

" When this wandering mind is brought to the abode of truth and His name becomes its life-breath, then God Himself guides and shows the way of unity. He who is sinless, even though leading the life of a householder, whose spirit is awake, the thirst of whose mind is quenched with the nectar of the name, the Guru shows him how to serve the True One and realise Him."

" How can anyone without proper preparation attain the unattainable ? " asked another.

" I never said that," answered the Guru. "The seeker after truth must prepare himself. He should not indulge in overeating or waste his day in sleep, but with a singleness of purpose concentrate on True One, permeated with the sound of the true word, freed from attachment and egoism, having banished passion, wrath, and pride, and with perfect self-control follow the Guru's instruction."

" Where is He hidden ? " asked another Sidha. " What is the meaning of emancipation ? How should an aspirant conduct himself ? "

The Guru said :

“ He is hidden in every heart.
He whom the Guru instructs is emancipated.
The uninstructed is born and dies.
The aspirant through the word,
Becomes one with the True One.
Swallowed by illusion,
Bound by ignorance,
The unawakened is lost.
By the Guru’s instructions He is found,
Darkness is dispelled, Egoism is destroyed
And the aspirant becomes one with God.”

“ Tell us more about it,” said another Sidha, who was listening with great attention.

“ He who rises above the three basic tendencies and treasures only the essence, the Lord leads and helps him to cross the ocean of life,” said the Guru.

“ You talk of a God with personal qualities and also without qualities,” asked another. “ Can you explain the mystery ? ”

“ The unchanging Absolute is without qualities and manifests himself with qualities. It is only by the grace of the Guru that the supreme state is reached and one is absorbed in the sacred word. It is then that this mystery is resolved. The aspirant should get rid of the ‘ I-am-ness ’ and the thought of separateness and concentrate on the True One.”

“ When an aspirant follows the instructions of the teacher, the lotus of his heart opens and is filled with love for all and in that overflow of love his ego is drowned and he realises reality. He is exalted who sees himself in all beings and feels for all as he feels for himself.”

“ If all are in Him, then why do only some attain salvation while others wander from birth to birth in this world of sin and sorrow ? ” asked another.

“ They who cling to the false and the unreal, they find not the true place. The come and go,” said the Guru. “ They who attach themselves to the True One, they blend into the True One.”

“ He who follows the True One’s way
He has perfect wisdom and eight-fold powers,
He crosses the troubled sea through right knowledge,
He knows how to discriminate between right and wrong,
He knows both the law of involution and the way of freedom,
He knows how to cross to the other side.
The body is the shop, the mind is the dealer
Salvation is obtained by dealing in truth.
Sayeth Nanak, the sacred word bestows the secret of salvation.”

“ You speak as if the path was easy and even a child could take it,” observed another, “ but the fire of desire is not quenched even by endless subjection of the body to discipline.”

“ Perhaps not,” said the Guru, “ but there is a simple way to quench it.

" Destroy the feeling of I-am-ness
And with it the sense of separation.
Destroy the sense of duality and attain oneness.
The path is hard for the ignorant and egotistic
But those who take shelter in the word, are absorbed in its essence.
He who realises that both within and without is He,
His fire is quenched by the grace of the Guru.
O friend, sayeth Nanak, destroy the poison of passion,
And the fire of desire and win the favour of the Beloved."

" How is the fourth state of consciousness reached ? " asked another.

" He the Absolute is within and without and in all the three states of consciousness ; he who attains the fourth state of consciousness realises Him. He knows the primal being above Maya, the spirit of self is absorbed in His name, he becomes one with God."

" You have said nothing about the ancient system of practising Yoga," asked another. " Don't you believe in its effectiveness ? "

" I have heard of the system, but I do not believe that merely by outer restraints Yoga can be attained. What is needed is inner change. Let the soul draw itself into itself, close the nine doors, no more run after sense objects, and take its seat in the tenth and hear the soundless sound, absorbed in the True One, see the True One in every heart, then the secret becomes manifest and reality is realised."

The Guru continued, " Evil thinking is destroyed only by dwelling on the word of the Guru, who alone can show the gate of salvation. He who remains unaware of the reality, continues to burn in the fire of desire. Separated by evil inclination, he suffers. Total submission to the divine will is more than all the knowledge and virtues, and complete self-surrender is the way to secure divine approbation."

" What do you mean by total submission ? "

" Total submission is entire freedom from subjection to the three Gunas and becoming an instrument of the divine will with a heart full to the brim with God and then the sense of ' I-am-ness ' vanishes and also the sense of separation."

" By what means does the mind remain stable ; by what food is hunger satisfied for ever ? " asked another.

" He who is the same in pleasure and pain has attained stability of mind ; he hungers no more. By God's grace death has no terror for him."

" How was the world created and how can its misery be removed ? " asked another Sidha.

" The world exists in I-am-ness, in forgetting Him is the suffering. By the Guru's instructions control of mind is obtained, and sense of ' I-am-ness ' removed. Righteous aspirations gradually gather the treasures of truth."

In general, the Yogis practised Pranayam and physical postures (asans). They tried to convert the Guru to their cult. The Guru, however, impressed on them the superiority of the ' Sahaj Yog ' which depends on an inner change beginning with ethical development in overcoming five passions, rising above desires and final surrender of the self and total submission to the divine will.

The Guru laid stress on the control of the activities of the mind, the cultivation of dispassion and the repetition of the name of God with the incoming and outgoing breath culminating in complete Samadhi.

36

THE GURU WENDED HIS WAY THROUGH ALMORA TO THE forests in area which is now included in the district of Pilibhit and reached another abode of Yogis. He sat at a little distance from their residence under an old tree which had dried up, but to afford shade to the Guru it instantaneously sprouted into green leaf. The Sidhas saw this and full of wonder approached the Guru.

" Ades O Bala—salutations, young man—"they said, " if you are an aspirant for Yoga, come and join us."

" Join you ! " said the Guru, " and put on rings on my ears and yellow robes. No, Yoga means union. It is not attained by smearing the body with ashes or carrying a club or donning the yellow robes. Nor it is attained by shaving clean the head or by blowing the horn. The secret of living and of Yoga is to be discovered by remaining in the world without being affected by it."

" You think anyone living the ordinary life of a householder can attain freedom ? "

" I am sure one can," said the Guru. " Yoga is not attained by dwelling in graveyards or cremation grounds or by sitting with closed eyes, nor by wandering in different countries or visiting places of pilgrimage. But its secret is discovered by remaining pure amidst the impurities of the world."

" How is it," asked a Sidha, " that all the people who lead the ordinary life of a householder do not become Yogis ? "

" They are not even seekers of truth," said the Guru. " It is only when a seeker meets the Guru, who dispels the darkness of his mind and its apprehensions and teaches control of the mind, that bliss untold is poured into the innermost core of the being and the secret of living in the world without being soiled by its contact is revealed."

" Has he to practise Yoga ? " asked the Sidha.

" He has to learn to die to the world while living," said the Guru, " and listen to the sound of the horn which blows without the blower and reach the stage which is not haunted by fear or desire,"

" You talk in enigmas," said the Sidha, " but you have said nothing to show that the life of a householder can be that of a Yogi."

" In simple words," said the Guru, " the vesture of the body and the symbols of denominations are of no account, nor does the desire die with leaving a household. The inner change, the true conversion, can take place anywhere, more likely under the stress and storm of the performance of ordinary duties of a householder, which constantly call for self-denials, than by abandoning the school of life and wandering into the desert lands of self-glorification."

37

THE GURU WAS PASSING THROUGH A VILLAGE, WHEN HE SAW a crowd gathered round a Sadhu, who was sitting under a village tree. Those who offered him some coins he invited to sit near him and on those who brought him nothing, he cast eyes of disapproval.

The Guru was amused. " Desire and aversion are with you still," he said. " Only a rare one gets freedom from these, hunger of the body and mind drive men to their doom."

The words of a true teacher have a strange way of entering hearts. Simple village folk turned to him as he spoke and sought his feet. " Teach us, O true teacher," they said.

" He who allows the wealth of his own soul to be robbed and cannot safeguard it, he has no right to cast a critical eye on others. Only he who under the instructions of the Guru tastes the nectar of God's name can guard the treasures of the soul.

" Listen, O people, and search your hearts. They who are attached to personal pleasure are unfortunate, they have closed the gates of the spirit : they will repent at the end.

" Desire can never find fulfilment ; defeated in the pursuit of sense objects, caught in the web of pleasure and pain, victim of circumstances, a man finds peace neither here nor hereafter. He who is no more troubled by the pairs of opposites, having taken shelter in God, is on the way of finding true happiness. He transcends life and death.

" There is nothing more satisfying than the nectar of His name. Those who taste it quench their thirst. He who deluded by illusion has not tasted it has missed the secret of retrieving the self.

" The body is sustained by a breath of air and is ruled by the mind. The divine spark is hidden in the soul. It is only by divine grace that the mind learns to turn towards God and taste the nectar of his name. It satisfies all hungers and the mind is absorbed in God.

" In the company of saints, arts of praising God is acquired. and the nectar of God's name is tasted, and by the grace of the Guru, the terror—the fear of death—is destroyed. O people, receive from the Guru the sacred name of God. He is indeed fortunate who is thus favoured."

This saying the Guru walked on but those who heard him were converted and became his disciples.

38

THE GURU THEN PROCEEDED TO PANIPAT AND SAT NEAR A well under a shady tree. Panipat was known to be the abode of Shah Sharf, who had attracted a crowd of holy men round him. One of his disciples saw the Guru and took him for a Muslim and saluted him. The Guru replied as usual by saluting the 'Alekh' the indescribable. The faqir did not follow the meaning of the word, but reported to his master that a holy man peculiarly dressed with two disciples had arrived and sat near their well. The curiosity of Shah Sharf was excited and he came to see the Guru.

" You seem to be a Hindu faqir," he said. " Why have you not shaved your head ? "

" Is it any use having the hair, when the mind is unshaved," answered the Guru. " A clean shave of the mind must precede a clean shave of the head "

" You are right," admitted Shah Sharf, " but which is the true path ? "

" The path of complete self-surrender," said the Guru. " He alone is worthy who becomes dust for the feet of the Beloved."

" What are the characteristics of a ' darvesh ' ? " asked Shah Sharf.

" He is a darvesh," said the Guru,
" Who, while living is dead to the world.
He is awake while the world sleeps.
Who permits his self to be plundered
And having lost all meets the Beloved.
Only few who seek His door are seekers at heart,
Who feel neither sorrow, nor joy, nor wrath, nor pride,
Who are unafraid, to whom gold is dross,
Who enjoy what is right and lawful,
Who have no other desire but to serve the Lord,
Who Self-restrained, chaste and true,
Control the five senses,
Who, established in the highest plane,
Are absorbed in the soundless sound.
Sayeth Nanak, neither the Vedas, nor the Ouran
Can know the greatness of such saints."

" You are indeed such a person," exclaimed Shah Sharf.

They continued their friendly discourse for a long time.

39

AT PANIPAT THE GURU HEARD THERE WAS GOING TO BE A very large gathering at Kurukhshetra, and thousands upon thousands of people were coming to bathe in the sacred tank and pray that the Sun might be saved from an eclipse.

The Guru decided to visit Kurukhshetra to draw the attention of erring humanity from the unreal to the real, from external ceremonies to inner purifications.

The Guru took his seat near the tank. A young prince who had been hunting in the neighbourhood had killed a deer, and, as he passed the Guru, he offered him a piece of venison. The Guru accepted it and asked Bala to cook it. Bala was surprised but obeyed the Guru. A great crowd gathered round him. This was a sacrilege, which had never been committed before, and on such a day when the Sun God was harassed by his enemies. He was besieged by angry Brahmins and others, who were ready to stone him. The Guru stood up and spoke and his words worked like a magic. The crowd stood spell-bound.

" I am doing this to show you," he said, " that this matter is of no account. They who harbour in their hearts evil thoughts and under the cloak of abstinence aspire to holy living, know not the truth. They who wash the outside of the cup, which is brimful with pride, wrath and hate cannot become saints till they empty it of these. Hypocrites do not find the gateway to the True One.

" Fools wrangle about eating meat.
They know not the truth, or the way of right action,
Or the difference between meat and vegetables,
And acts that are sinful and those that are sinless.
They in ancient days killed rhinoceros
And offered its flesh
In oblation at the sacrificial fire.
They the man-eaters, pitiless and cruel,
Hold their noses and forswear flesh
Is it any good telling the blind
Who cannot see or act upon what is right ? "

" You call those who disagree with you blind," exclaimed a Brahmin with deep resentment.

" They indeed are blind," said the Guru, " who act blindly, whose hearts are unawakened ; they who would see their parents starve and do nothing to relieve them but raise their voices in holy horror if anyone eats meat.

" Man is born of flesh, nursed in flesh, is a tabernacle of flesh. Men call themselves Pandits without knowledge and without doing what is right. The eating of meat is sinful, but gratifying of greed is held good. All living things are of flesh and have their being in flesh. They who follow a blind teacher eat eagerly what is unlawful and refrain from that which is lawful. Men and women seeing each other become slaves of lust."

The words of the Guru, in some strange way, possessed the mind of the crowd and they felt what they had never felt before, that the Guru had revealed the truth that it is more important to banish cruelty from the mind than abstain from eating meat.

" You care for the shell and disregard the spirit," continued the Guru, " for you untruth has become truth. Lead a righteous life and serve others. Such is the true path. If anyone salutes another, let him salute in the name of the Creator—Kartar—and respond in the same manner saying ' Sat Kartar ' —' God is the only truth.' "

They who came to stone the Guru became his disciples and established a Dharamsala, wherein God's name could be recited and the weak and weary could find shelter.

40

THE GURU BY SLOW STAGES, AFTER VISITING MANY VILLAGES and towns on the way, and instructing all those who came in touch with him, at last reached Hardwar. He proceeded to Kushwant Ghat, where a crowd of pilgrims led by priests were performing various ceremonies to obtain salvation for their dear departed ones. 'Har-ki-Pauri' had not then acquired its present importance.

He saw a multitude of people offering water towards the sun with their right hands. He moved forward, stood facing the priests and began to offer water towards the west and with his left hand.

One of the priests moved forward and said, "You fool, what are you doing ? Come, I will help you to do what is right."

"I am doing just what you were doing," replied the Guru, and continued offering water towards the west.

"We are offering water to the departed," said the priest, "to quench their thirst.

"Then I am offering water to quench the thirst of my land," said the Guru.

The priest laughed and said, "How can water from here reach your land in the Punjab ?"

The Guru stopped, as a crowd had gathered round him. "If the water I throw cannot reach my land, which is on this earth, how can the water you throw reach the *pitries* (ancestors) who are no more of this earth and no more troubled by the hungers of the body ?"

"How stupid you are," said the priest. "It is by the power of Mantras that the *pitries* receive what is offered. We hold this supreme secret. You cannot water your fields by splashing water from here. Come, do something for your *pitries.*"

"You trade on the credulity of men and women." said the Guru. "You know that you know nothing. You have forsaken the right path and claim to secure paradise for those that are gone, by throwing water toward the sun and other useless ceremonies. You have forgotten the Creator and his sacred name. How can those who have not saved themselves save others ? You are preparing yourself for hell."

The simple truth struck home. The crowd for a while stood spell-bound and then an old priest strode forward. "How dare you speak like this ? It is you whom hell will claim. You who bear no caste marks and look neither a Hindu nor a Muslim. We are Brahmins and worship gods and godesses as ordained. We are custodians of the divine secret. We follow what the Shastras ordain."

The Guru sweetly smiled and said, "Anger is not the attribute of those who follow holy scriptures. The custodians of truth must have control over their senses. They who perform ceremonies with no love of God or man in their hearts and receive money in return are doomed. Learn to worship God, to love His creation. The door to paradise cannot be opened by splashing water but by selfless action and by absorption in the Sacred Word."

The crowd listened with rapt attention and the priests retreated, leaving the Guru, who took his seat at a place which is now called Nanak Bara and is occupied by Udasees.

The Guru sat surrounded by pilgrims, calmly instructing them in the ways of truth, when one of those persons who always ask questions and never follow the truth enquired, " What is superstition ? "

" I will show you," said the Guru. He got up and approached a Brahmin who had drawn a circle round him and was cooking his food.

" May I come within your circle," asked the Guru, "and take some firewood ? "

" Get away," he shouted. " If you step within my circle you will pollute my food."

" This is superstition," proclaimed the Guru. " The Brahmin yonder has drawn a circle and considers that by so doing he is keeping out impurities. He is refusing to admit people of lower caste than himself, but he has all the polluting influences about him in spite of his circle. What can be more polluting than evil-mindedness, cruelty, a slanderous heart and the fire of anger ? These are with him in spite of the circle."

" Teach us the true way ? " they asked with folded hands.

" Listen," said the Guru full of joy. " Draw the circle of truth, self-restraint and good acts around you and occupy the seat of truth. Bathe in the pool of sacred Name. They indeed in the next world take the high road who on earth shun the way of sin."

41

FROM HARDWAR THE GURU SLOWLY TRAVELLED TO Allahabad, where the Kumbh fair was about to take place at the time of a conjunction of the stars which occurred every twelve years.

He was passing through a village when he came across a crowd, where some Muslim faqirs were discoursing on religion. The Guru joined them and after a while they invited him to speak.

The Guru said, " It is not speech but righteous living which can light up the path of religion. Listen :

" In the first place
Remove from the mind
Feelings of attachment, self-aggrandisement and harmfulness ;
Attachment to family, attachment to action.
With freedom from attachment all shadows will disappear.
He alone is established in truth
Whose heart is imbued with truth,
Who has washed away the dirt of untruth,
And by removing impurities has become pure."

After giving the advice the Guru resumed his journey. The Guru reached Allahabad and took his seat near Sangam, the junction of the two rivers Ganga and Jamna where at the appointed time great crowds swarmed to bathe. The Guru remained seated and made no attempt to bathe. A Mahant who watched him was shocked at his behaviour. He approached him.

" Are you demented ? " he said. " Why don't you get up and bathe ? This opportunity will never occur again."

" What opportunity ? " asked the Guru

" The opportunity of washing away your sins," said the Mahant.

The Guru said :

" They are not pure who wash their bodies :
They indeed are pure in whose hearts He dwells."

A crowd gathered round the Guru and he continued :

" They who come to bathe in holy water
With minds full of deceit
And hands ready to steal. The outer dirt may be washed by bathing.
But they increase the inner dirt twofold
Like a brass vessel that is polished without
But is full of poison within.
The saints are pure without bathing :
The thieves remain thieves in spite of bathing.

Next to where the Guru sat, a Pandit with his body smeared with sandalwood paste displayed his idols on a small *chowki*. He sat with his eyes closed and only opened them when someone made an offering to the idols.

The Guru was greatly amused. " What do you see when you close your eyes ? " he asked.

" In my *Samadhi*," replied the Pandit, " I see the three worlds. Please don't disturb my meditation." Thus saying he closed his eyes.

The Guru asked Bala to remove his *chowki*. When he opened his eyes again he found his *chowki* gone.

He turned to the Guru and asked, " Tell me who has stolen my *chowki*."

" Close your eyes and find it," replied the Guru.

" Please do not torment me," he pleaded almost in tears.

" I will not," said the Guru. " Your *chowki* is safe, but is your soul as safe ? " You are a learned man, and yet in spite of your learning, you stoop, for the sake of a few pice, to deceive others. My friend, collect the wealth of the sacred Name. Save yourself and save others. Listen :

" He indeed is a fool
Whose mind thirsts for money,
Who laments when money it lost.
Only rare ones gather the true wealth,
The wealth of the sacred Name,
Inspired with true devotion.

They are drenched in the colour of the sacred Name.
They offer their mind and soul to God
And take refuge in Him."

42

FROM ALLAHABAD THE GURU PROCEEDED TO BANARES, KASHI, which was said to be the abode of Shiva. It is believed that anyone who dies on its sacred soil goes straight to heaven. It was, and still is, a great seat of learning.

The Guru sat near a famous ghat. His garments which were neither those of a householder nor of a sanyasi and his Hindu and Muslim companions attracted attention. A couple of learned Pandits came to him to hold discussions on various systems of philosophy.

"Panditji," asked the Guru, "how does a sinner by merely dying here attain salvation?"

"He who touches the garment of Shiva becomes pure. A sinner no more remains a sinner when he reaches Banares."

"You are learned in the six systems of philosophy," said the Guru. "Does anyone who reads or listens to the recital of Patanjali Yoga, become a Yogi and acquire powers?"

"No," said the Pandit, "only practice of Yoga endows a Yogi with power."

"Does it not follow that salvation cannot be attained by dwelling in a place but by working for it? Just as a Vedantin does not become Brahm by the mere assertion that he is a Brahm."

"Tell me then," said the Pandit. "We read the Vedas and acquire knowledge. Why does our knowledge not blossom and ripen into flower and fruit?"

"You read and you recite but you rarely realise truth. Mere lip service is of little avail. You never grasp even the real import of words you read. Then you perform endless ceremonies to secure enjoyment and greatness and feed the fire of desire, thus sowing fresh seed of Karma, but you make no attempt to be one with Him, by serving His creation. Every selfish action forges fetters and binds the soul to the cycle of birth and death. The recitation of Mantras, the repetition of the Sacred Name impelled by whirlwinds of desire is of no use in the wilderness of the world. As long as passion, attachment, hate and pride preside, the reading of the scriptures and telling the rosary are of no avail. It is like clinging to a carcass which is without life. Listen," said the Guru, "I will teach you the right way.

"Worshipping a stone God,
Displaying a rosary of sacred beads,
Is like watering a barren soil.
Why waste life in empty formalities
And plaster the body from outside
When it is crumbling from inside?

Fill the mind with charitable thoughts,
Make a raft of the sacred name,
Become bountiful and cross the ocean of life.
Make thy body like a Persian wheel,
Harness thy mind to its yoke,
Draw the nectar and irrigate the soil of the mind.
Change passion and anger into digging tools
With them rid the soil of the weeds.
The deeper you dig, the greater will be the harvest.
Thus learn the art of spiritual husbandry.
Honest labour earns its reward.
Even a heron by divine grace can become a swan.
Thus prays Nanak, thy humble devotee,
Bestow thy bounty, O bountiful One ! "

The Pandit asked, " You speak as if you know all, but have you read the Vedas and Shastras ? "

" Listen to the truth," said the Guru :
" A man may carry a cart-load of books
He may have books all around him,
He may carry books in boat-loads,
Or fill empty caves with books,
He may read books for months and for years,
He may read them throughout his life,
Till breath leaves his body.
Nanak sayeth only one word is of account
All else is for the glory for the self."

" Do you hold then that the study of Vedas and Shastras is of no use ? "

" It is of no use unless what they teach is practised. They are like beacon lights in surrounding darkness. Would it help a man who has lost his way to gaze at the light without taking the road which the light is destined to show ? "

" How can one take the right road," asked the Pandit, " without proper exploration ? "

" Dispel the darkness of 'I-am-ness.' It is the root cause of hope and fear. Listen :

" When a true teacher is found
Real peace is gained
And God's name enters the heart.
Hope and fear depart.
The sacred word destroys ' I-am-ness.'
By divine grace this gift is granted."

The crowd that had gathered treasured every word that the Guru uttered. They felt as if they understood that the ego was the centre and the source of attraction and repulsion, of suffering and pain, hope and fear. The ego escaped from these by submission to the divine will and gained freedom by absorption in His name.

There gathered round him a group of Sanyasis and they pressed him to become a Sanyasi. The Guru answered them in a hymn :

" In ignorance they leave their home
And then visit the homes of others.
Having run away from the duties of a householder
They are lost in the whirlpool of desire.
Without meeting a teacher,
They wander about and read books,
Whetting the edge of desire.
Without knowledge of the word
They fill their bellies like animals,
And remain unprepared.
A Sanyasi, if he is absorbed in the word,
Which the teacher gives him,
Crosses the three worlds.
He who dips his garments in a vat of ochre
And wanders in the garb of a beggar.
He who tears up his clothes and makes a bag,
To receive offerings from others
Wandering from door to door and pretending to instruct
The world of blind men
Without knowledge of the word,
Cheated by superstition, like a gambler,
He loses the game.
Unless a sense of discrimination is awakened,
The inner fire is not quenched
With austerities.
The fire of devotion is not kindled
Without serving the teacher.
How can he know the self
Who makes a hell for himself by slandering others ?
Atman is unable to reveal itself to a darkened mind
Wandering in sixty-eight places of pilgrimage
Lost in superstition, how can he wash away the dirt of desire ?
He who sifts ashes and powders himself with them,
Still in pursuit of sense objects on the path of illusion,
Not knowing what is within and without,
How can he discover truth ?
Reciting and reading sacred books

Enveloped in darkness with no sense of truth ?
Shaving the head or growing matted hair
Keeping silent and nursing the ego
The mind wandering in all directions
Undipped in the vat of self-knowledge
Drinking poison, with no thirst for nectar,
Mad with the wealth of the world
Self-willed and without good action
Such a one is still in an animal state.
Carrying the beggar's bowl,
Mind obsessed with hunger of desire
Having abandoned one's own wife,
Seeking another man's wife, driven by passion,
Without discipleship and knowledge of the word,
Treasuring poison under the cloak of external renunciation—
The angel of death will take such a one to task.
Such a one is lost in this market place of the world.
He is a Sanyasi who loses himself
And follows the true teacher.
Who is not worried over daily needs
And remains undisturbed by desire.
Who does not talk nor indulge in vain speech,
Who enjoys the wealth of contentment,
Who dispels the darkness of the mind by the sacred name—
Blessed is a householder more than a Sanyasi or a Yogi
Who is devoted to the feet of the Lord
Undisturbed by desire, the true Renouncer
Remains absorbed in thoughts of Him
Drinking the nectar of God's love
Concealed in the innermost recesses of the soul.
He permits his mind to wander no more
Static and unmoved under the Guru's instructions,
Untiring in his search of truth,
Such a one possesses the wealth of the Name."

FROM BANARES BY SLOW STAGES THE GURU REACHED GAYA, associated with the name of Lord Buddha, but a stronghold of Hindu priests, who declared that any offerings made at a particular place on the river secured absolution for seven generations for those who had departed from the earth.

They professed to feed *pitries* (ancestors) by offering rice-balls, they lighted up little lamps to illumine their path in the high heavens and performed prolonged ceremonies.

The Guru stood on the banks of the river Sarju and watched them. He suddenly burst into a loud laughter.

The priests engaged in sólemn ceremonies were surprised. " What are you laughing at ? " they asked angrily.

The Guru said, " Do you not see how ridiculous your ceremonies are ? They who have left this body, do they need food, do they need a glow lamp to see, where neither the sun nor the moon shed their light ? They see without sunlight just as you see without light when you dream."

" The essence of food reaches them and the lamps we light illumine their darkness," asserted the priest. " Come, do your duty to your forefathers. Tell me the name of your village and I will find your priest."

" I make no such offering and light no lamps," said the Guru :

" Brimful with the oil of suffering is the lamp (of life)
Kindle the flame of the Name,
The flame of the sacred Name
Will consume the oil of sufferings,
And the Lord Himself will be seen.
Don't you, O people, scoff at what I say
A spark can ignite and consume
Logs stacked in their thousands.
The rice-balls placed in a leafy platter
Of what avail can they be ?
The only means of salvation is the name of God
In this world and the other it is our only sustenance.
In His adoration the *atman* finds joy.
For they whose hearts are steeped in the ocean of the name
Bathing in Ganges and Jumna is of no use.
He indeed is made clean by bathing
Who adores Him night and day.
The Brahmin makes rolls,
Offers them to *pitries* (ancestors) and to God,
But eats them himself.
Sayeth Nanak the roll of divine grace,
Is every where and for ever satisfying."

The truth of what the Guru said touched their hearts, but the priests were frightened that people would desert them and follow the Guru :

" You are not wiser than the sages who gave us the scriptures. You are criticising in the light of human understanding, but what the scriptures teach is beyond the bounds of human understanding."

" You follow the scriptures when it suits you," answered the Guru. " You follow what is convenient and profitable but you shun the call for sacrifice. Do your scriptures recommend indulgence in lust and greed ? If you are learned in the scriptures, tell me, what is truth ? Point out the difference between the path of darkness and path of light. You are not only untrue to yourselves, but you mislead others. You prevent people taking to the right path by showing easy methods of salvation. All such acts are sinful. How can you help those who are gone, when your own actions are not free from sin ? "

" Take thyself away," said the priest. " We do not enter into argument with ignorant rustics."

The pilgrims however entreated the Guru to enlighten them further. " Judge for yourselves," said the Guru. " When the material body is no more, how can it require material things ? If this body cannot go to the other side, how can any material things of this earth reach the spirit ? In the true name of God is hidden the secret of salvation for the living and the dead, only its light can illumine the darkness of the earth and provide guidance in the high heavens. Make a boat of the sacred name and with the oars of faith cross this ocean of illusion."

The pilgrims paid their homage to the Guru and implored him to stay. He remained with them until a few pure souls were converted and then resumed his journey.

44

THE GURU WITH HIS FOLLOWERS WAS PASSING THROUGH THE forests of Assam and his followers were unable to secure any food. Mardana one day in despair exclaimed, " You, O Guru, are of God, the formless, neither hunger nor thirst affects you. I am a mere mortal man. I must have food."

There was a soap-nut tree nearby. The Guru turned round and pointed out, " Go and eat its fruit, but remember you are not to bring any fruit with you."

Mardana was aware that soap-nuts are not edible. They are bitter and unpalatable. At the same time he was aware also that the Guru never uttered a word that was not true, so he followed the Guru's instructions, picked up a nut and put it into his mouth with some hesitation and found it sweet. He then climbed the tree and ate the nuts till his appetite was satisfied. He then forgot the Guru's instructions and collected and carried some with him.

Next day when he again felt hungry he started eating them and found the fruit so bitter that he began vomitting and almost lost his voice.

The Guru laughed, "This happens when greed prevails. You would not share nuts even with your friend Bala." The Guru touched Mardana, and he recovered his voice immediately.

In this place a temple has been built, the soap-nut tree still exists and its fruit is gathered by pilgrims, who distribute it to their friends.

The Guru stayed for a day there and here a group of Yogis headed by Bhartari came and resumed their discussions in the hope of converting the Guru.

"Ades, O Nanak," said Bhartari by way of greeting him.

"Ades, salutations to Him," said the Guru, "who is true in all ages, over-existent and beyond the bounds of time."

Bhartari came and sat near the Guru. "Why do you wander like a Yogi, and refuse to enter our fold ? Come, I will put ear-rings in your ears, clothe you in the garments of a Yogi, make you a perfect Sidha and instruct you how to live for ever."

"What ! Is it necessary to pierce my ears to make me a Yogi ?" asked the Guru greatly amused. "I thought Yoga was the union of the individual spirit with the divine spirit and not a matter of a change of garments. My friends, outward forms and physical exercises are of no use as long as the ego rules. Make your mind free of egoism, pride, attachment and anger, before you begin teaching others."

Bhartari was annoyed. He, the witness of ages, to be questioned by young Nanak. "Listen," he said, "I inherit the wisdom of centuries, our system has endured from the beginning of time and its truth has never been challenged."

"I beg you not to be annoyed," said the Guru. "Age is no evidence of the intrinsic merit of any system. Have not good and evil existed side by side from the beginning of time ? Your system does not eradicate the five evils : passion, anger, greed, attachment and desire."

"Have you any real power beyond words ?" said Bhartari.

"None," said the Guru. "I can do nothing against the law of God. It is only He who can perform a miracle."

"Bah," said Bhartari. "You see my disciple sitting in front of you, watch him. He will rise up to the skies, and become invisible in a moment. If you have any power, bring him back to earth."

The disciple in a moment flew upward, and was soon out of sight. Bhartari turned to the Guru, and said, "Find him."

"Hide and seek is the play of children. Wait and see," said the Guru. As he said this, his two sandals flew upwards and after a short while, they saw the disciple descending and the sandals beating him down. Bhartari and his followers could not stop the beating. In an instant the disciple fell at the feet of the Guru.

Then all of a sudden the Guru disappeared from amongst them and Bhartari himself went in search of him. After a long time he returned and confessed his inability to find the Guru. "I have searched the earth and the water and the high heavens," he said, "but I cannot find the Guru." He had hardly said this when they found the Guru seated in his former place amongst the others.

"Where did you hide yourself," enquired Bhartari full of astonishment.

"I was with you all the time," said the Guru. "The body dissolved itself into its elements and the soul in the all-soul."

The Sidhas were overwhelmed with awe and sat spell-bound.

The Guru said :

"Fill the mind with the word of the Guru
Put on the garments of forgiveness
Submit to the will of God, unmoved by pleasure and pain,
Thus the treasures of *Sahaj yoga* are gathered.

The soul bound on the wheel of birth and death
From age to age wanders in its thirst for things.
The immortal name gives the release
And confers knowledge leading to realisation.

Discard discussion and abide in the divine abode,
Listen to the unceasing soundless sound,
Lose thyself in its music,
Listen to the Divine horn that is blowing.
Charge thy mind with discrimination,
Awaken wisdom with the stick of knowledge.
Smear thyself with the ashes of all that exists.
Recite the praises of God, this is the path of the Guru.

The one light is in all forms
In innumerable forms and species
Realise Him in the whole universe—
Meditate on the supreme Brahm, O Bhartari."

The Sidhas were overcome by the truth of the Guru's teaching and fell at his feet.

45

THE GURU BY DESIGN LOST HIS WAY AND FOUND himself in a thick forest, which was infested by a tribe of Bheels who ate human flesh. The Guru travelled many a weary mile. He was never affected by physical infirmities but his two companions were tired, hungry and depressed and at their request the Guru sat under a tree. Mardana was hungry and after a little rest started to find something to eat.

The Guru warned him, "There are wild men living in this forest, so be careful where you go."

"You are Nanak Nirankari, God's own," said Mardana. "You are not affected with hunger and pain. I am a mere man and subject to both."

Mardana had gone a few furlongs, when Kauda, a notorious Rakhshas, met him. Kauda kept oil boiling in a big pan to roast his victims. He saw Mardana from a distance. He was delighted at the prospect of a good flesh. He took Mardana by surprise and in an instance trussed him with rope that he carried. Kauda then carried him to spot where his pan was boiling.

Mardana now prayed to the Guru to save him. The Guru already knew of his distress and was on his way to help him. He arrived just at the time when Kauda was preparing to throw him into the boiling pan.

Kauda stopped as he saw two men approaching him. He thought he had two more victims. He rushed towards them swinging his rope.

As he approached, the Guru raised his hand and Kauda stopped dead trembling from head to foot and then fell on the ground unable to move looking helplessly with his large wild eyes at the Guru and entirely bewildered. Bala released Mardana.

Then the Guru turned to Kauda and commanded him to rise. Kauda slowly raised himself and then fell at the feet of the Guru and prayed for mercy. He said, " It has been foretold that a man of God will save my soul."

" God is all-merciful," said the Guru. " He is all compassion. He forgives all those who repent and abstain from doing wrong."

" I will do as you bid me," said Kauda. " Accept me as your disciple."

" Listen," said the Guru, " and act on what I tell you and thus win grace. Learn : attachment, greed, anger and harmfulness are the four streams of fire. These consume mankind. Only virtuous action can quench the fire and open the treasures of bliss.

" From now onward resolve to harm no one, be merciful and serve all those who need your service. Concentrate your mind on the Creator, learn to love him with all your heart and mind, just as lovers do, and make His name the sustenance of your life."

Kauda was converted completely and to the end of his days acted as a devout disciple of the Guru.

46

FROM JAGANNATH PURI THE GURU CROSSED OVER TO Assam and reached the place where there was a temple of Kamakshi Devi in Kamroop. It was the seat of black magicians. The temple was in charge of the Queen of Kamroop. She herself and all her companions practised black magic and exercised superphysical powers. The Guru and his companions made themselves comfortable under a tree, but Mardana went forth to see the town and to procure some food. He had not gone far when he encountered a party of three gaily dressed women, who asked in their language, " How and why have you come to our town ?"

Mardana answered in his own rustic Punjabi, which they could not understand, and his costume and ways amused them. " He bleats like a lamb," said one of the women.

The other woman laughed and said, " I will make him into a lamb " and thus saying she took out a thread, breathed something over it and threw the thread on the neck of Mardana, and then commanded, " Now become a lamb and bleat."

Mardana instantly stood on all fours and began to bleat. All the three women clapped their hands and burst into laughter.

In the meantime the Guru saw what had happened to his companion and immediately started to save him from his tormentors.

When the women saw the Guru and Bala coming, they were greatly amused. " We shall turn all these now into animals," they said. " I will make that young man bark like a dog."

She approached Bala and was going to put the thread round his neck when the Guru said, "Become that on which your thoughts are fixed."

The woman at once went on all fours and began to bark like a dog.

The Guru directed Bala to remove the thread from the neck of Mardana and asked him to utter Satnam and sprinkle some water on Mardana which he did and immediately Mardana stood up and wiped the beads of perspiration from his face.

The second woman attempted to throw a rope round the neck of Bala, but as she lifted her arm, it remained fixed in the position in which she was aiming. The third woman moved to her assistance but found that the jar she was carrying over her head was fixed as if by cement.

A fourth woman saw what had happened and ran to the Rani to report that a great magician had arrived who rendered their powers useless.

The Rani herself came to the spot and in all sorts of ways tried to work her magic, but to no avail. She could not cast a spell on the Guru or his companions, nor could she release her three women. A great crowd gathered round them and all were terrified by the power of the Guru.

The Rani then bowed before the Guru, placed a pile of gold and jewels in front of him and prayed, " O great magician, accept me as thy disciple, teach me thy magic, and release my sisters."

The Guru told her to take away her gold. The Rani then fell at his feet and prayed for mercy.

" You ask for mercy and it will be shown to you. You must promise to abandon your wicked practices of black magic and seek refuge in God." Thus saying the Guru uttered Satnam sprinkled a little water on the three women who were restored to their normal condition.

" See, your goddess has given you the power of doing mischief without any power of healing suffering hearts."

" You are great," said the Rani. " You are saying what is true."

" God alone is great," said the Guru, " who creates, maintains and withdraws this universe unto Himself. We suffer when we follow the wrong way and do evil ; when we turn to Him and follow the golden rules of life, we become virtuous and earn its reward in happiness."

" Maharaj, we have been misled. We have followed the traditions of our tribe."

" That is why I have come to you to lead you to the right way," said the Guru. " Listen :

The light of the Lord shines
When we turn our minds to Him.
When we discard evil doing,
And do what is good,
Misery vanishes,
And is replaced by happiness.
Nanak says serve Him
By whose service all suffering is destroyed
He is the giver of all things."

The Guru then instructed them in the first place to purify their body and mind by dethroning hate, covetousness and jealousy from their minds and replacing these by sympathy and love. "Become queens of mercy," he said. "Man is always going astray. You can make a paradise for him on earth and help his ascent by your own example, by holy living and the magic of self-surrender. You can open for him the gates of Heaven by your own devotion. You can teach him the meaning of love by your own selflessness. You are goddesses in your own right, worship no ugly images, but fulfil your divine mission to sow in the hearts of boys and girls the seed of virtue and teach them by your own living that courage and truth are rooted in their being. No syllable of religion is ever understood but through a virtuous deed."

After a short stay the Guru departed leaving behind him an aroma of peace and awakened souls to carry on his mission.

47

FROM GAYA THE GURU PROCEEDED TO JAGANNATH AND towards the evening he entered the temple and sat in one corner of the inner court. As soon as the sun set, the priests and pilgrims gathered in great numbers and performed *arti* (evening ceremonial service) by burning incense and blowing conches, ringing bells and waving lights which were carried in a salver. The Guru never moved and took no part in the ceremony.

"Are you ill ?" enquired a priest approaching him when the *arti* was over. "Why did you not join in offering *arti* to the Lord ?"

"Where is the Lord ?" asked the Guru.

"Are you blind ? The statue of the Lord is before your very eyes ?"

"Am I blind ? Tell me how can a statue of wood represent the Lord of the universe ? He who is beyond human imagination. He is boundless. He the all-pervading."

"Beware what you say," shouted several voices.

"I speak the truth," exclaimed the Guru. "The lord of the universe does not dwell in wooden statues crudely sculptured by carpenters. The Lord of the universe dwells in every heart. He pervades all that is and the whole universe worships Him. He the unknowable, the all-merciful, the creator, I worship and perform his *arti*."

" How ? " asked the crowd.

" Listen," said the Guru, and he began chanting. Mardana played the *rubab*. The temple was filled with the music of his voice and that of the *rubab*. The whole crowd stood spell-bound with their hearts drawn towards the invisible God, in a state of rapture, taken out of themselves by words that entered the heart and commanded acceptance.

" In the salver of the sky,
The sun and the moon are the lamps
The luminous stars are the pearls
The warm wind from the Malaya mountains
Wafts the incense.
The god of air waves the Chanvar
The forests of the world offer their wealth of flowers
And the spheres play their music.
Thus is Thy evening service performed,
O Thou destroyer of suffering.
A thousand eyes are Thine.
No, no, Thou hast no eyes.
A thousand forms are Thine.
No, no Thou art one without form.
A thousand stainless feet are Thine.
No, no, Thou art without feet.
A thousand scents are Thine, that pervade the universe.
No, no, Thou art without scent.
In everything is Thy light.
It is Thy light
That illumines everything.
It is by the grace of the Guru
That the secret light is found.
What is pleasing to Thee
Is the best of the evening service.
Day and night my heart thirsts like the bumble-bee
To touch the dust of Thy lotus feet.
And may thirsty Nanak
Like the chatrak drink the nectar
Of thy grace
And devote every breath to Thee."

When the Guru stopped, the crowd, including the priests, in spite of themselves, fell at his feet. After a momentary pause, the Guru addressed the congregation :

" The Lord of the universe is not confined in one place, house or temple. The sky, the earth, nay the whole universe with all the plants and millions of stars and earths and suns and moons are His. He is all-pervading. He creates and He, in destroying, recreates. There is no end to His greatness. The whole universe bows before Him. It is His light that is in the sun and the moon. It is His light which is in each of us. Seek it within your hearts. It is manifested in the Shabad, the name. Therefore take refuge in the sacred name, charge every breath with His name till elf is submerged in its sound and through His grace salvation is attained."

The Guru, having instructed the people, walked out of the temple followed by the pilgrims, Mardana asked for some water to drink. The Guru stopped where he stood and said "Dig where you stand and you will discover a spring of sweet water."

Mardana obeyed and the other people joined him and after some digging, a spout of sweet water flowed forth near the sea and the whole crowd drank from it. This spring still flows in the *dharamshala* which the disciples of the Guru built round it.

The Guru stayed for three days and instructed the people and when on the third day he was about to depart, the people asked him to give a parting message.

Thus spoke the Guru :

"Act in the light of *Buddhi*, the higher wisdom, and follow the path of righteousness, control the five senses and restrain them from the pursuit of sense-objects, keep a vigilant watch on the mind, lest the fire of desire consumes the self. Above all, take refuse in Him and invoke His name. He is pleased when in others we see the face of a brother and extend the help which we wish others to extend to us. The more this feeling of fellowship grows, the nearer we draw to God. There is no other way but this, that we learn to love one another and thus find the secret of loving God."

48

THE NEXT PLACE THE GURU VISITED WAS KANCHI. IT HAD two temples, one dedicated to Shiva and the other to Vishnu. They both had stone idols of gods.

The Guru stood at the gate of the temple and watched the procession of pilgrims taking their bath and then entering the temple with flowers to offer to the idols.

A priest approached him and said, "Have you not found your priest ? Come, I will guide you."

"No, I want no priest," said the Guru. "I am marvelling at the ignorance of the priests and of pilgrims."

"What do you mean ?" asked the priest.

"I mean that the priests are failing in their duties. They ought to instruct the pilgrims. They are only interested in relieving them of their money."

"Shut up," shouted the priest.

In the meanwhile a crowd had gathered round the Guru. "Your ears cannot hear the truth," sweetly remarked the Guru, "that is why you fail in performing your *Dharma*. You who ought to be the teachers have become consciously or unconsciously charlatans.

" Bathing in holy rivers
Only removes the dirt of the body.
The body gathers dirt again.
Bathe in the pure stream of knowledge
Which makes both body and mind pure.

Why worship gods and goddesses ?
What can you ask of them ?
What can they give ?
The idols that you bathe and worship, O brother,
Sink in the water.
How can they help anyone to cross the ocean of life ?

The world is steeped in ignorance,
And has no sense of true values.
The unknowable cannot be known,
Without the instructions of the true teacher.
The hand of the Lord, O brother,
Holds all boons.
He exalts.
He gives to whom he pleases."

The pilgrims were much impressed. The Guru talked in the language which they understood, while the priests talked in a language which some of them themselves did not understand.

Sadhus, priests and Pandits gathered round the Guru. A learned Pandit approached him and asked, " Out of the six schools of philosophy which do you follow ? "

" There are six schools, six teachers, and six are the teachings. The Lord is one though seen in different garbs. The house (Shastra) in which the Lord is praised is worthy of respect. Moments, minutes, days, weeks and months are made by the sun. The sun is unchanging while the seasons change. Nanak says the Creator appears in many garbs. The teachings that awaken adoration of the Lord are the only ones worth following."

" You talk as if you knew all," observed the Pandit, " but you know not a word of philosophy. You cannot understand the deep knowledge that lies hidden in our sacred books, nor you can understand the significance of pilgrimages." The Guru said :

" He is learned indeed
Who does good to others.
The test of learning is action.
He indeed performs a pilgrimage
Who controls the five passions.
He indeed dances with joy,
The music of whose anklets,
Makes the mind one-pointed.

He is a Sanyasi
Who is without hope or fear.
He who has no fear of death,
Is a Yogi perfectly harmonised.
He indeed is a naked faqir
Who has subdued his own self
Who harms no living thing
And overflows with compassion.
Thou, O Lord, appearest in diverse vestures
Nanak cannot describe thy play."

The people implored the Guru to stay and he acceded to their request and instructed them in the path of discipleship.

49

THE GURU THEN TRAVELLED FURTHER SOUTH AND AT LAST reached Rameshwar. He did not go to the temple but sat outside on the seashore. There were *sadhus* in groups, some with their families and children occupying various halting places.

They were greatly intrigued by the appearance of the Guru and his two companions. They could not place them under any denomination. The Mahant of one of these groups could not suppress his curiosity. He approached the Guru and asked, "To which denomination do you belong ? What is your name ?"

"My name is Nanak Nirankari, and I belong to the denomination of the Formless," he answered.

The Mahant was struck by the youthfulness and saintly expression of the Guru's face and decided to convert him.

"My good boy" he said in coaxing tones, "there is something in you that attracts me. Come and be my disciple and some day I will make you the Mahant of *vairagees*. I will place Thakurjee (the idol) in your keeping,"

The Guru smiled and said, "How can you place the Lord of all creation in my keeping ? He in whose keeping is the whole universe."

Listen :

"In the light of the true word
Suffering is destroyed.
He who serves the Guru,
Can know the Lord."

"Thakurjee is the symbol of the Lord ; in worshipping him in stone we recognise his presence in all things," said the Mahant.

"He is in all things," said the Guru, "but all things found manifestation through the word and it is through the sacred word alone we can reach Him."

A great crowd of women and children gathered round the Guru.

" Dear friends," said the Guru," recite the sacred name, seek the true guru and see with your own eyes the Lord."

" You lay down the law," said the Mahant, " as if you saw the past, present and future. Tell me what holds the whole creation ?

" The tentacles of attachment enmesh all creation. Salvation is attained by freeing the self from attachment. Listen : Father and mother, son, daughter and wife, daughters-in-law and their children are chains that bind mankind. The cultivator who produces and contributes to the revenue of the State, the trader who works for profit and the banker who hoards money are all bound by attachment. All actions, all duty performed in the interest of self, all reading of holy scriptures to aggrandise the self become the cause of bondage. These increase the sense of selfhood. There is no escape from bondage," sayeth Nanak, " without taking shelter in the sacred name, devotion to God and protection of the Guru."

" Maya," continued the Guru, " deludes the self in infinite varieties of ways, by attachment to relatives, desire to accumulate wealth, and ambition to become powerful and great. The soul of man thus forges fetters which hold him to earth. It is only when the illusions of Maya fade and obssess the mind no more, that truth is realised and the soul of man finds refuge in God."

" How can a man seek salvation without performing good actions such as the worship of idols and the performance of ceremonies as laid down in holy books ? " asked a Pandit who had come to listen to the conversation between the Guru and the Mahant. " By abandoning these we seal our own doom."

" You are learned in the ancient lore," replied the Guru. " Look within your own heart and admit that these acts are inspired by desire and forge the chains of Karma which hold the soul to the cycle of birth and death. The truth is :

The will and desire make the chains
Actions, good and evil, tie up the knots.
These sustain the world.
All actions spring from desire.
The world is deluded by Maya.
Listen, O Pandit, absorbed in the performance of ceremonial acts
The only act that secures true happiness
Is contemplation of His divine essence
Without the sacred name we work our own doom."

" You seem to have no regard for the teaching of Vedas and Shastras." quoth the Pandit with anger. " It is not right to listen to your seductive speeches."

" I speak the truth," said the Guru. " What is the good of your talking about the teachings of Vedas, when you ignore their teachings and perform acts that bind the soul ? The dirt of sensuous acts is not removed by mere performance of ceremonial acts. You weave like spiders the web that entangles others and destroys them and yourself."

" I cannot listen any more to you," said the Pandit rising. " You are an iconoclast. Men like you are enemies of ancient *Dharma* and should be shunned."

The crowd that had gathered round the Guru, beseeched him to tell them more.

" There is nothing more to tell," said the Guru. " One word of truth is enough if you treasure it in your hearts. It has the power to convert the soul from selfhood to selflessness. Listen :

Misguided intelligence
Points out many paths
Leading the mind to the wilderness.
Without the true teacher
The Light of the sacred name
Remains undiscovered.
And, without it, darkness
Of the mind is not removed.
It is when the true teacher bestows the sacred name,
That the cycle of the coming and going is closed.
The Guru sows the seed of truth
In its sprouting the mind is purified,
And filled with truth.
He who devotes himself to the Guru
He receives the gift of knowledge.
Without the Guru the true path is not found.
They who are driven by greed
And perform formal acts, O brother,
Are cheated by untruth.
They dope themselves with the drug of ceremonial act."

The Master continued :

" If we churn the curds
We produce its essence : butter.
If we churn water we produce nothing.
This is the substance of truth.
Without the Guru, doubt is not dispelled,
And the Infinite dwelling in every heart discovered.
The world is like a cotton thread
Enmeshing all things within its net.
The Guru alone can untie its knots.
All other acts are of no use.
This universe is cheated by desire :
What else can one say ?
When the Guru is found
Fear of God enters the mind,
The reality of death is realised.
The value of virtuous deeds is recognised,

And the power of the sacred name.
He who is guided by the Guru
Is given the gift of the sacred name.
He is freed from all worldly formalities.
The body is like a jeweller's shop
Stock it with the jewel of the sacred Name.
He who stores the Guru's sacred word
Stocks this merchandise.
Blessed is the trader who trades in it."

The audience were so impressed that they showered flowers on the Guru. In the place where the Guru sat, a temple has been raised in his memory and still exists on the seaside.

50

IN SANGALDEEP THERE LIVED RAJA SHIVE NABH, WHO WAS anxious to tread the path of discipleship. His friend Bhagirath, a trader from India, and a disciple of the Guru, had told him all about Guru Nanak, his wonderful power of leading people to the true path and conferring salvation. The Raja asked Bhagirath how he could meet the Guru.

He replied, " If you concentrate your mind and with purity of heart pray for his presence, he will not fail to fulfil your true desire."

Eevery morning Shive Nabh prayed earnestly for the Guru to reveal himself to him in person. He was told that the Guru enjoyed staying out under open skies, so he planted a grove of shady trees for the sojourn of the Guru. Many persons came and stayed in the grove and claimed to be gurus and were found to be charlatans. Days ran into months, months into years but there was no trace of the Guru. Shive Nabh almost lost hope of seeing the Guru and neglected the grove and some of its trees began to shed their leaves and were withering.

The Guru with a group of disciples stood on the seashore at Rameshwar and said, " A friend of mine is waiting to meet me on the other side. I must go across and gratify his devoted longing.

" How can we do so ? " asked the disciples.

" If the sacred name has the power to enable all men to cross the ocean of death, that name can take you across this small span of water. Utter *Waheguru* repeat the one *omkar*, the true word, the creative spirit, free of fear and hate, timeless, birthless, self-existent. " This saying the Guru walked over the surface of the water and asked others to follow him. Bala and Mardana obeyed. The waves were hushed and opened a path for Guru and he moved as swiftly as if the air itself was carrying him and his followers to the other side.

In due time they touched the land and the Guru walked to the grove which Shive Nabh had dedicated to him. As soon as he entered the grove the withered trees sprouted into green foliage.

The report reached Shive Nabh that a holy man had arrived. He had been deeply disappointed by men who wore various garbs of holiness but were unredeemed within and deceived others. He now followed a well-conceived plan of testing the merits of his visitors, so he ordered two of the prettiest court dancing-girls to visit the Guru and tempt him with their wiles and if they failed to seduce him, he would then visit the holy man himself.

The girls almost danced into the grove dressed in gay garments full of laughter and mischief, carrying baskets of flowers to offer to the Guru, sure of conquest, proud of their beauty and the magic of their passionate music to enchant him, as they had done in the case of many a wandering anchorite. As they entered the grove an indescribable calmness possessed their minds and robbed them of their artful ways. They walked humbly to the place where the Guru sat, bowed to him in all humility and sat respectfully at a distance from him. The sweet music which Mardana was playing accompanied by the Guru who was singing, entered their hearts and chased away evil thoughts. They sat spell-bound like statues. The Guru sang :

" O my mind, love the Lord
As the lotus loves the water.
The waves dash against it
But its love is ever increasing.
O my mind, how can thou find release
Without love to open the inner door
To receive the treasures of devotion ?

O my mind, love the Lord
As the fish loves water,
The deeper it dives the happier it is.
Its body and mind are at peace.
It cannot live a moment without water.
So must thou live in the Lord—
He is aware of thy travail.

O my mind, love the Lord
As the *chatrak* longs for the rain.
Though lakes may be overflowing
And the land green with verdure
Its thirst is not quenched
Without a rain-drop from the sky.
True love only grows on the soil of good action.

O my mind, love the Lord
As water loves milk.
Place it on the fire, it burns itself
But protects the milk.
He unites the separated selves,
He exalts the true one by His own grace.

O my mind, love the Lord
As the *chakvi* loves the moon
And the whole night

Calls for her mate from afar,
Who is near, Minds possessed by self are never conscious of Him.
They whom the Lord enlightens are always in His presence."

They who heard the hymn were held by the words of the Guru and not only were their bodies motionless but their minds were calm. The news reached the Raja that those whom he had sent to tempt the new arrival had passed under his spell. The Raja hurried to the grove and found the gates closed against him. He humbly prayed to be forgiven for his trespasses and to be admitted. The prayer was heard and the gate opened of itself. The Raja entered and fell at the feet of the Guru.

" Teach me, O Lord," he said, " I have waited for you for countless years."

The Guru asked him to rise. " I have come in response to your steadfast devotion," he said, " I knew you were waiting for me."

" I have waited long," repeated Shive Nabh. " Now you have come and all my longings fulfilled."

" Driven by desire," said the Guru, " men calculate their gains. They do not realise that things happen as He ordains. The whole world values the transitory, and does not realise the value of the reality. When true teaching reveals the reality, only then is the truth discovered and the treasures of peace gathered."

" How is it," asked Shive Nabh, " that men wander without true devotion and fail to follow the right path ? "

" Only the pure in heart can follow the path of devotion," said the Guru. " It is an act of complete self-surrender to the Lord, its reward is the wealth of knowledge of all that is in the three worlds. He who is seeker of virtue never forgets the true name."

" This world has an appearance of permanency," observed Shive Nabh, " and yet all that exists is in a state of flux."

" Even those fluttering birds who feed on pearls of knowledge from unfathomed depths have to depart. Everyone has to depart and may be called in a moment and leave this playground to-day or to-morrow. He whom the Lord saves by His grace meets the true teacher and he retires victorious."

" How is it that fire of devotion is not kindled in every heart," asked Shive Nabh.

" Without the true teacher, said the Guru, " the dirt of desire is not destroyed and devotion does not possess the mind. Devotion unlocks the secret of the word. *Soham* is revealed and with it knowledge of the self. A righteous man acquires knowledge of the self. Nothing else is of any account."

" Do the devotees find union with the Lord ? " asked Shive Nabh.

" Yes," said the Guru, " through the power of the word they are in Him and need no uniting. The ignorant know not this truth and as separated selves suffer again and again. There is only one gate and one house. There is no other place."

It was about sunset now. The Raja begged the Guru to come to his palace. The Guru acceded to his request. Next morning the Raja and his wife, Rani Chandra Kala, came to the Guru.

The Rani asked, " From your dress, it is difficult to judge whether you are a monk or a householder. Are you a Pandit, a Yogi or a householder ? What path do you follow ? "

" I follow the path that leads to God," said the Guru with an indulgent smile. " There is no other but the Lord who must be loved. Men follow many paths driven by desire and wander away from the true path—the path of Love."

" Are you a Yogi ? " asked the Rani.

" He is a Yogi who knows the secret of the pure name. By its power he is made pure. He who loves the Lord, the true one, becomes one with Him, and transcends the bounds of life and death.

The Lord has no name or caste. He is a Pandit who is soaked in knowledge of God and worships Him by ever singing his praises. He invokes the One Name—one God, and sees one light in all the three worlds.

He indeed is a householder who holds the scales even and whose tongue utters the name of the Unknowable. There is one dealer, one Lord of all, and His customers are also of one kind only. Their minds are free from delusion and they realise Him and become one with Him, and their cycle of birth and death is broken by the true Guru. They are full of the word, free of all delusion, and day and night worship the Lord by serving His creation. God's light is reflected in the form of Guru and his teachings illuminate the seekers. Through his teaching God is realised both by a Pandit, a Yogi, a householder and a Sanyasi. Nanak has become such a one and crossed the ocean of Maya."

" Forgive me, O true Guru," she said. " I am asking questions which people generally ask to resolve doubts. Your words are like shafts of light which dispel darkness.

From where does the soul of man come and where does it go ? What is its source and to what does it return after death ? How is it bound ? How is it freed ? How does it become one with the Eternal ? "

" It comes from the Eternal and returns eventually to the Eternal," said the Guru. " Its source is the eternal consciousness and into eternal consciousness it returns. Attachment is the bondage. By righteous living the bondage is loosened. By exalting the Lord's name, the sacred word enters the heart and flows like nectar leaving no room for the darkness of desire and then the human soul becomes one with God.

" Like birds that flock in the evening on a tree, flutter with pleasure and pain, scan the skies morning and evening, wandering everywhere, driven by hunger, so the soul of man wanders and suffers on earth.

Those whose hearts are captured by the sacred name, their minds freed from the poison of hate and desire—their hearts empty of evil—to them the Guru opens the closed gates of true vision.

" Purity of mind is the result of past meritorious acts which bring the soul in touch with the true teacher, who opens the gates of everlasting bliss. Those who submit their will and their body to God are worthy of reverence."

During his stay at Sangaldeep, the people of the town profited by the teachings of the Guru. The Guru had noticed that the Raja, the Rani,' and a few others were anxious to hear about the practices of the Raj Yoga. The Guru gave his teachings in a long poem called ' Ratan Mal Ramkali ' He held that a seeker of Yoga must begin by securing seclusion where he can meditate without interruption. He must subdue the five senses, eat little, sleep moderately, dwell constantly on truth and by restraints of the body and mind awaken higher centres of consciousness.

" He who has brought the five senses under control," he said, " who never speaks untruth, who has brought the five passions, seven impediments, and nine gates under subjection is on the path of attainment. Out of millions who strive only a rare one acquires the knowledge of the true one. The Yogi leads his consciousness to the innermost recesses of heart, and from there to the hidden brain-centres, where the three streams meet between the eyebrows. He draws the power that pulsates through the nerves known as Ida and Pingla, from the right to the left and unites them so that they become one. It is thus that his vision broadens and he sees far away the goal and beyond it the supreme point is difficult to attain. His consciousness then perceives the nine spheres and all that exists in the four quarters, east, west, north and south."

" It is all so difficult," said the Raja. " Tell me some simpler way."

" Make this body the container," said the Guru." " Pour into it the milk of human kindness. Leaven it with true aspiration and convert it into curds. Make discrimination the churn and the sacred name the churning rope and churn again and again and collect the butter. This is the way of Yoga."

" Pray, tell me more about it," said the Raja.

" A Yogi must rid himself of the darkness of desire and greed and allow the five passions to burn themselves out. He should keep the bow of true resolve constantly strung to destroy the self and its evil thoughts. He who repeats no other Mantra but God's name, in him righteous tendencies grow strong and evil tendencies die of attenuation. He is never caught in the noose of death. Such is the characteristic of a true Yogi.

" He finds the right way to practise the sacred name and, when practised with skill, it bestows perfection. Without skill it is unproductive like a barren woman. Conquer the mind and with the dagger of knowledge destroy the five passions and place the wandering mind under restraint. He who learns the art of subduing the mind becomes an Udasi."

" Hom can we know a Yogi ? " said the Raja.

" He who is restrained, to whom gain and loss are the same, who neither rejoices nor sorrows, who does not waste his powers by clinging to earth, but keeps the kite flying upward till in the innermost recess of the brain the spirit buzzes like a bee. This is the characteristic of a Yogi.

" He is a Yogi who speaks of nothing else but of true knowledge and of God and whose awakened consciousness is absorbed in meditation, throwing strings of devotion into the fathomless, to form a link with the Absolute. His lips no more express the sorrow of separation. Adoring the Lord, he by the grace of God becomes one with Him. Even lesser gods bow in obeisance to him ; such are the characteristics of a true Yogi."

After staying a few days more and giving true teachings to both the Raja and the Rani, the Guru left Sangaldeep.

All the people of town became his disciples.

FROM SANGALDEEP THE GURU ACCOMPANIED BY BALA AND Mardana proceeded to Kanya Kumari and on arriving there sat on a mound near the temple of the goddess. He was not there for long, when he saw a large crowd hurrying with offerings to the goddess. The priests had given out that the goddess was angry and people from all the neighbouring villages came to propitiate the goddess with their offerings. Some of them came to the Guru and begged him to accompany them and intercede on their behalf.

The Guru laughed and said, ' O ye people' why are you afraid of gods and goddesses and not afraid of Him, who has created the universe. You think you can propitiate the stone statue by your offerings, which are of no use to the idol. Learn to be afraid of Him who sees all your thoughts and actions and metes out utter justice. In His court men are judged by their actions, the righteous find favour and are freed and the unrighteous reap the harvest of their own sowing. He is formless, the true, the unchangeable, and the real who pervades and transcends all that is. Learn to live in fear of Him. Listen :

In fear fire performeth its forced labour,
In fear winds and breezes blow.
In fear flow a hundred thousands of rivers,
In fear the earth beareth its burdens,
In fear Indra moveth unceasingly,
In fear sitteth Dharam Raj at the gate ;
In fear is the sun, in fear is the moon.
They travel millions of miles without end.
In fear are the Sidhas, the Budhas, the demi-gods
In fear are the stars and the firmament ;
Warriors and mighty men and divine heroes
In fear, streams of men
Flow from the unmanifest to the manifest.
God hath destined fear for everyone
Nanak, the formless, the true one alone is beyond fear."

The audience stood spell-bound. The power of his words was such that it possessed the hearts of men. The crow swelled by new arrivals and men prayed to be instructed. The Guru spoke in the language of the people he addressed.

" Listen," said the Guru, " do not let your spiritual emotion run to waste worshipping stone gods and goddesses. Worship Him, the Lord of all creation. He is not to be won by offerings. He demands complete purification and dedication of body and mind. You worship Him when you are aware that He is in all things. When you see Him in all beings you begin to love His creation and love one another. Then all quarrels, wars and cruelties come to an end. Earth is His kingdom. Joy and true happiness are His gifts. He is within you. Make your hearts pure, repeat His name and lose yourself in adoring Him."

The audience requested further enlightenment. " Listen," said the Guru :

" He is indescribable, boundless, immeasurable
He is not subject to time or death
He is neither in high caste nor in low caste
He is unborn, self-existent, He has no attachment or aversion.
I am a sacrifice to that true one,
Whose action are also true.
He has no form, colour or mark.
The true word is his only symbol.
He has no mother or father, nor wife, nor relations,
He is free from all desire.
He is beyond intellect, beyond all Maya.
Beyond all and everything.
His light is in all directions.
In every being is Brahm hidden,
In every heart is His light.
Under the instruction of the teacher,
Closed gates are flung open,
And undisturbed Samadhi is attained.
All creation exists in time,
Takes birth and dies,
As ordained by Him.
By the grace of Guru
The key by the true teacher is given.
By the magic of the word emancipation is obtained."

" It is only when the vessel becomes pure that it is filled by the true one.
There is one in millions who knows the mystery of self-surrender, and thus
becomes one with the Supreme," sayeth Nanak, " and then the human soul
becomes one with Supreme soul."

They who listened were converted to the truth of the Guru's teachings and
became his disciples. They agreed to discard the worship of other gods and
goddesses except the one supreme God.

52

THE GURU THEN PASSED THROUGH THE PROVINCE WHERE THE matriarchal system prevailed and reached the town which was the seat of the ruling Queen. The Rani was learned in the lore of Hindu religion. She was not only learned but was charitable. She had built a *dharamshala* where strangers and holy men were welcomed and entertained.

The Guru, as was his wont, stayed in a grove of trees outside the town. The news was carried to the Rani that a holy man had arrived. She was busy performing *havan* and sent a messenger to invite the Guru to the *dharamshala*.

The Guru thanked the Rani for her invitation and said he was happy where he was.

The Rani, as soon as she had finished the ceremony, herself came to the Guru. She considered it a privilege, and her duty as a ruler, to meet holy men and to entertain them. She bowed respectfully and said, " O good Sir, why have you refused my hospitality ? Am I unworthy to serve you ? Is my food unrighteously earned ? "

" Nay," said the Guru. " You are worthy in every way. You gather your revenue and return it like rain for the benefit of your subjects. He who earns and gives away knows something of the way. He who does not appropriate everything to himself but gives and induces others to give in the name of God is blessed. He who shares his bread with others knows the law of living."

" Is it not all an illusion ? " asked the Rani. She was well-versed in ancient literature. " What is Maya ; is it real or unreal, *sat* or *asat* ? "

Ah ! my daughter," said the Guru, " is your mind entangled in the web of these speculations ? Only he who sees both the real and unreal can speak with authority. Listen :

All His regions and His heavens are real.
God's world and all His creation is real.
All His thoughts and acts are real.
All His laws and His judgments are real.
All His commands and decrees are real.
All His graces and symbols are real.
Real is His power, real is His might,
All that is manifest and is seen is real.
Millions upon millions declare Him to be real
All His praises and powers are real.
Nanak says they alone know reality
Who meditate on the true one."

" If I have understood your meaning," said the Rani, " you hold that Lord, the Creator, is real and, therefore, his manifestation cannot be unreal."

" Raniji," said the Guru, " it profits little to dwell on these theories. Know that He is real, pursue the path of righteousness and get established in reality. They who dwell on the ever-changing, fascinated by the ever-changing, remain subject to birth and death."

" The learned," said the Rani, " the great Pandits expound theories which it is difficult to follow, but what you say seems true."

" Raniji," said the Guru, " there is only one thing needful, learn to mould the mind so that it becomes fit to receive the divine light. Listen :

They who clothe themselves in pure white,
With minds, dark with evil thoughts,
And claim equality with those,
Who stand serving at the door,

They make fair show in speech,
But indulge in evil action.
They who are absorbed in the Lord
Imbued in His bliss, having attained power,
Are humble and meek.
Make thy life worthy by joining such devotees.

Discussions about realities are beyond the region of human intelligence and mere discourses on religion are of no avail unless virtuous actions purify the mind and make it fit for the realisation of truth. When darkness of the mind is thus removed, it is only then that the light of spirit can illumine it and in that light is seen the difference between the real and the unreal. By becoming one with the real salvation is obtained."

The Rani bowed, perfectly satisfied. She had ordered food which was brought by her servants. The Guru got the food distributed amongst the poor who had assembled outside the garden. The Rani was deeply concerned as the Guru distributed the food, for he was keeping nothing for himself.

The Guru read what was passing in the mind of his hostess. He turned to her and said : " My daughter, you were pouring oblations into the sacrificial fire. Learn that *havan* such as I am performing is twice blessed for I offer food to the Lord by appeasing the fire of hunger of his children."

The Guru stayed for many days and was visited by rich and poor alike. The Rani asked him one day, " What is the object of life ? How should one live ? This wandering mind is difficult to control."

" There is no other way but to dedicate all actions to the Lord and to carry out His will, when desire to serve Him fills the mind it awakens true devotion. Listen :

He alone lives
In whose heart the beloved dwells.
No one else tastes the reality of life.

They who have no place
For God in their hearts
All their acts bring pain.
They whose lives are harmonised with God
Whose consciousness is aware only of Him
They alone truly live.
The whom the self holds down to earth
Are subject to death.
They who surrender the self to God
Ascend to the realm of bliss."

The Guru then sang the following hymn :

" When we forget the beloved
Even for a passing moment
The mind is filled with suffering.

If the Lord does not dwell in our hearts
How can we find admission to His presence ?
When the true Guru is met
The fire of desire is quenched
By the waters of virtue.

O my mind, night and day
Dwell on the greatness and goodness of God.
They who never forget Him
Even for a moment
Such men are few in this world.

When light mingles with light,
Human consciousness with divine consciousness,
Becoming egoless and harmless,
All doubts, fears and sufferings disappear
By the grace of the Guru.
God Himself dwells in the devotee's heart.

O devotee, subject thyself to Him
So that he, the enjoyer, may enjoy.
Why attach thyself to that
Which is passing ?
He becomes the favourite of the Lord
By the grace of the Guru
Who is absorbed in His service.

Destroy the four fires
Drench them in the water of God's name.
Then the heart will be filled with nectar
And the immortal lotus will bloom.
Seek and serve the Guru,
Truth will dawn in thy heart,
And bring thee to the presence of the God."

53

FROM KANYA KUMARI THE GURU VISITED THE FAMOUS temple of Sri Rangam built on a small island in the middle of river Kaveri, covering a large space with its courtyards and its massive buildings, crowded with *sadhus*, pilgrims and wandering bulls.

Here, and there sat *sadhus* and Pandits engaged in hot discussions about different philosophies, each upholding his own cult and waxing wild in discussion.

The Guru stood and listened and then said, "You hold discussions about that which you have not seen or realised. Your mind is as disordered as the surroundings in which you live. It is a case of the blind leading the blind."

"How dare you intrude in our learned discussions," exclaimed the Pandits angrily, "and declare that we know nothing. We, who are learned in all the Vedas and Shastras, know all that can be known."

"If you had realised Him, my friends," quoth the Guru, "you would have understood me and remained silent. It is an empty pot that makes a noise, when it is full it is silent."

"You talk as if you know more than we do. I am sure you could not interpret a single sentence of holy scriptures," said the Pandit.

"I can interpret the condition of your mind," said the Guru with a smile. "All your learning has not taught you the control of hate and anger. Conceit holds you in subjection. How can you even speak of God when these fill your mind ?"

"Are you a monist or a dualist ?" asked another.

"The question has no meaning for me. I am neither a monist nor a dualist. I am a devotee of the Lord, a suppliant at His door ; to be one with His creation and with Him is my goal."

The crowd left the Pandits and gathered round the Guru and begged him to instruct them. The Guru then recited a hymn to the assembly.

"Listen, my brothers. The panacea that can cure all the ills of the world, the Guru only can give. Discard these disguises of various creeds, worldly cleverness and doubt-creating discussions. These can bear no fruit. Fix your mind on God and allow your mind no more to wander. You follow the path of pain, when you seek in externals the path of peace. The cure lies hidden within. The way to discover the amrit is to cease to do evil, to do good, abandon vice and acquire virtue, for vice is the cause of suffering. They who cannot discriminate between right and wrong, sink deeper and deeper into the quagmire. Bathing in holy waters is of no avail when the filth of falsehood and greed fills the mind. The heart becomes pure when it receives the Guru's word and treasures it. You must first drive out from your mind covetousness, slanderous thought and speech, and untruth. It is only then that the word of the true teacher becomes significant. Surrender yourselves to the Lord. Adore His name and pray, Keep us, O Lord, as thou willest."

The Guru then entered the temple ; many people followed him. He found the priests rubbing a piece of sandalwood on a block of stone, to make the sandalwood paste to put on the image.

The Guru broke into a hymn :

"Rub the tablet of the mind,
With the sandalwood of His name,
Mix it with the water of good actions,
And breathe into it the sacred name.
Without the sacred name,
It is not possible to worship.

Why wash the body from outside ?
Wash the mind,
Clean it of the dirt of desire,
And tread the path of salvation."

The Guru stayed for a few days and led many a seeker after truth to the right path.

54

THE GURU CONTINUED HIS JOURNEY, HALTING IN VILLAGES and towns and instructing all those who came in contact with him. In due course he reached Dhakni Onkar, a place of pilgrimage on the banks of the river Narbada. He found a large crowd bathing in the river and flowing in and out of the temple of Onkar. He stood at the gates of the temple and watched the crowd and his heart was filled with compassion. He sat near the temple and began to chant this hymn :

> " Just as you enter this temple and leave it, so men leave and enter the world. They are born again and die. They indulge in passionate enjoyment and sink deeper into the morass of the world.
>
> " They are proud of their bodily strength and their worldly possessions. They spend their energies in pursuit of women and gold. They thus themselves sow the seed of suffering. They forget God and are the victims of delusion.
>
> " They come to this temple to acquire merit, but they pass in and out without learning to exercise self-control. Without cultivating truthfulness, restraint and tranquillity of the mind, the demon of self operates in their bodies driving them to their doom. Remember without purity, charity and meditation, the wastes of life cannot be redeemed.
>
> " Why, O brothers, are you driven by greed ? Why don't you seek freedom from the cycle of birth and death ? Wordly possessions are of no avail. Death is sure to overtake you in your mad pursuit.

A great crowd gathered round him as he continued to speak. " What good is it bathing in waters considered holy when day and night you slander others and your mind is bankrupt of mercy or compassion ? You are making meshes of the net stronger that holds you on the plane of suffering with your own hand. You are caught in the web of attachment and sin. You appear in various disguises like an actor to allure others, only the true word can retrieve you.

" You suffer from the chronic disease of selfhood which is nursed by evil tendencies. It can only be cured by the word of the true teacher when discrimination is awakened by the true name. You feel happy as you survey your growing possessions and increasing comforts, but when you lose these you grieve. These are His gifts distributed by His grace. He who gives takes these back. At death nothing accompanies the departed. He, the primal being, is beyond all thoughts. Take shelter in Him.

" Foolish men attached to family, home and possessions pursue the unreal and lose the real. Death swallows them like a python. Why wail for the dead ? The dead cannot hear. We come under His command. We depart under His command. Forgiveness is of God.

" Seek the clue in the company of those who have tasted the alchemy of the Name. They can awaken wisdom and show the way to attain salvation. He who is not affected by pleasure or pain and is indifferent to the pleasant and unpleasant ; he who by subduing the self finds God is gathered unto Him.

" Happiness is not to be found in that which is changing. If we love the perishable, it must perish and separation and deprivation must cause pain. Outer ceremonies cannot cure the disease which is within you. Drink the nectar of the name to cure the sickness of the soul."

The crowd stood spell-bound, for the words of a prophet have power to enter and posses the soul. The people begged the Guru to stay and instruct them. The Guru agreed.

Next day he noticed the chief priest busy writing. He stopped and said, " Listen, O Pandit, what web of words are you weaving for the entanglement of the soul ? "

The Pandit looked up and was impressed by the glory that hung round the Guru.

" Tell me what should I write ? " he asked.

" Write the name of God," said the Guru, " who is great, who is true, the defender of the defenceless."

" We must remember," said the Guru, " that kings and nobles with all their possessions, and wandering faqirs possessing nothing, all speed away without house on the path of death, heavy with the burden of ill-deeds. The path is long, steep and beset with pitfalls, and unless the burden of sin is lightened by virtue no one can reach the haven of peace. They who spend all their days in accumulating wealth when the soul departs, they leave it behind and carry the burden of their deeds."

" The picture you have painted is so true. Tell us how to lighten the burden," cried out several voices.

" Acquire the wings of virtue in the days that are given to you. Lead a harmless and righteous life. Righteousness opens the gateway to realisation. Replace lust, wrath, covetousness and evil thought by dispassion, desirelessness, forgiveness and love. In this way remove the evil that clouds the consciousness and discover the difference between the real and unreal. Then control the mind and allow it to wander no more. God's first manifestation was sound. It is from sound that the whole universe flowed forth. Therefore the sacred word is the only manifestation of God. Charge every breath with the sacred word."

" You have not told us how *gyan* (knowledge) is gained," said the Pandit.

" He who cultivates virtue, receives the gift of knowledge," said the Guru.

The fruit of virtue is *gyan*. Remember lust and anger destroy the body just as borax turns gold into liquid. Millions upon millions have perished under this spell.

" Greed and egoism are evil. They who flatter and they who slander are untrustworthy. They are ignorant and without knowledge. Silver and gold are poisonous and perishable and men spend their days collecting them.

" He is not found by saying : He is not this. He is not that. Salvation is not obtained without following the true path."

" This mind is as restless as quicksilver," said the Pandit. " How can it be brought under control ? "

" It is true," said the Guru. " This mind never remains still ; it runs away like a deer. It is only by withdrawing it from the unreal and fixing it on the Lord that it can be brought under control. One must control the mind and keep it fixed. By fixing the mind on the Lord, one escapes death and learns to live in contact with the ever-conscious and imperishable. It is only then that everything, both real and unreal, becomes visible and happiness is attained.

" He the Creator is permanent. He is the giver of all things. Take shelter in him. This dreary path of hope and fear can be crossed by knowing the self and dying while living."

They said, " O true Guru, tell us the object of life in this world."

The Guru said, " Man comes to this world to gain emancipation, works like a drudge and is cheated beyond measure. He does not realise that he can gain true wealth only by treasuring the jewel of the name.

" On this earth overcome the mind, and remain day and night attached to God. He is the Lord of all, pervading the three worlds and the four ages. Having established the universe he remains unattached and unaffected. He is neither born nor dies. He remains unmoved and performs no acts. He is in all that is seen and unseen. Having created everything. He is concealed in every heart. He has no form or action. He is in the air and water and all that is."

" How is it that we cannot see Him ? " asked a simple villager. " We continuously hear that He alone exists, that the whole universe is under His command, and yet how is it that we do not realise this ?"

" Though all speak of the One, they realise not Him, because of the clouding of the mind by the darkness of self-assertion. When the barriers of self are broken, He is seen within and without and reality is realised. He is not far. He is near. He pervades the whole creation. He is the one Omkar, there is nothing else. The one who pervades everything.

" He who created the universe without any effort, His light pervades all the worlds. Read and understand and realise the truth. He, the true one, is within and without. When by the favour of the Guru the power of discrimination is awakened we know that the world is without any reality without him. Then we know how to gather the pearls of real value."

" There are various theories about the creation of the world so complicated that it is difficult to understand. Do us the favour of giving a clear exposition," asked another.

" The intellect cannot grasp what is beyond the bounds of intellect," said the Guru. " Rise above limited human consciousness and you will know something about creation. At present it is enough for us to know that the upper and lower regions are illumined by His light and His consciousness pervades the three worlds. He manifests Himself in forms and through his grace the soul of the universe returns again home. The sound of the word rains continuous nectar. The word is the only means of attaining perfection. He who knows this secret becomes one with the Creator."

" You have spoken of the power of the word," asked the Pandit. " Tell us what that word is."

" The unmanifested," said the Guru, "manifests Himself in sound—Shabad—and from Shabad the whole creation flows forth. Shabad, therefore, represents Him in this world. The way to Him is through the Shabad :

" The Brahma, the creator.
Was created by Omkar.
From the word Om again,
Came the universal mind.
From the word came forth time
And the limit of ages.
From the word came the Vedas.
Salvation is found
In the word Om.
The righteous disciple
Crosses the ocean by it.
Meditate on the word Om—
In the word Om
Is the knowledge of the three worlds."

55

THE GURU WAS PASSING THROUGH A VILLAGE, WHEN A devotee approached him and begged him to partake of his humble fare. The Guru accepted the invitation. He had hardly sat down to dine when a Brahmin approached him.

" Don't eat," he exclaimed. " This house is impure A son has been born in this house, and thirteen days of segregation are not over."

The Guru however had his meal, washed his hands and then turned to the Brahmin. " Listen," he said :

" Impurity of mind is covetousness.
Impurity of tongue is untruth.
Impurity of eye is to look with evil intent
On the wife of another, her beauty and her riches.
The impurity of the ear is to hear
Evil spoken of others

Says Nanak, he who harbours ill feeling
Goes straight to the realm of death.
Superstition is the source of weakness
It turns the mind to other things.
Birth and death is the law of life.
O brother, we come and go according to Divine command.
Eating and drinking is pure.
Enjoy the gifts of God.
They who follow the Guru's instructions
They and their homes are never impure."

56

THE GURU WAS PASSING THROUGH DELHI ON HIS WAY TO Mathra and Rajputana, and he rested for the night near an elephant stable. Suddenly he heard loud wailings which continued throughout the night. Early in the morning an elephant driver came to him and fell at his feet.

" O holy one, " he said, " I am ruined, my elephant died suddenly last night. I loved the animal. My children loved him and now I shall be thrown out of employment and my children will starve." Thus speaking he began to weep.

The Guru was touched by the grief of the elephant driver and his love for the dumb animal. " Go," he said, " say *Satnam*, touch the forehead of the animal with your hand, and say ' Rise'."

The elephant driver obeyed and, to his surprise, when he said *Satnam* and put his hand on the elephant's forehead, the huge animal shivered and came to life.

The elephant driver and his family were filled with joy, and the news that the dead animal had been restored to life spread like wild fire and people came to see the elephant. The news reached the King, Sikander Lodhi, who refused to believe it and came himself to verify the fact. He was surprised when the elephant raised his trunk and saluted him. It was his favourite elephant. He was led by the elephant driver to the place where the Guru was seated. " O holy one, how did you breathe life into the dead animal ?"

" I am of no account. It is only He who takes away life and restores it again."

" Can He take away life now ? " asked the King credulously.

" Perhaps, if you pray to Almighty, he may listen to your prayers," the Guru said.

The King prayed and the elephant sank back and died.

" O great one, restore the elephant to life again," asked the King.

" O foolish King," said the Guru, " it is only He who can reanimate the dead. There is no other but God. His will be done. You were His instrument in praying for the death of the animal. Iron when heated in the fire becomes red and the hand cannot hold it for a moment. Men of God become red with compassion in the heat of His love and cannot be compelled into that mood again."

The King bowed his head and placed large offerings in money before the Guru.

"These are of no use to me," said the Guru. "I hunger for God, my wealth of love has no attraction for you and what you have has no attraction for me. God has quenched all my hungers while the fire within you grows the more it is fed by worldly possessions."

"Bless me, O great one," beseeched the King.

"He is blessed who makes his heart a temple for divine grace to enter. Sow no more the seed of cruelty ; for what we sow we reap. Become a shadow of God on earth and serve His creation in faithfulness and truth. God's blessings will descend upon you."

In the meanwhile the Guru was surrounded by Qazees and Pandits, who invited him to discuss religious and philosophic problems.

"How can I discuss truth amidst pervading hypocrisy and with men whose intellect is clouded by pride and falsehood ? Listen :

They who profess to be religious
Indulge in sinful acts.
They who profess to teach
Hasten to the homes of disciples,
Instead of the disciple
Seeking the teacher.
Even the love of husband and wife,
Depends on what the husband can give.
No one believes in holy scriptures
Everyone worships his own self.
The Qazees occupy the seat of justice
They tell their rosaries,
And repeat the name of God.
They accept bribes
And in the name of Law
Administer injustice.

The Hindus seek
Relief from Muslim domination.
People slander and make false charges.
And injure others.
The Hindus clean the kitchen with cow-dung
As a mark of purity.
The Yogis grow their nails
And display matted hair.
They smear their bodies with ashes
And scatter their offspring all around.

Yoga is not attained in this way,
Not by covering the hair with ashes.
Learned men knowing,
The answer to their questions
Put questions to others
Such is this dark age (Kalyug)."

Then the Guru left Delhi. A sincere seeker followed him and when the Guru rested under a village tree, some distance from the town, he begged to be instructed. The Guru said :

" He who seeks the truth,
Keeps the fast of contentment,
Bathes in the sacred pool of meditation,
Makes compassion his God.
Forgivness his rosary,
Such a one gains favour of God."

The Guru said again :

" Wear the lion-cloth of restraint.
Draw round you the circle of true desire,
Put on your forehead,
The mark of good deeds,
And enjoy the repast of devotion.
A rare one experiences
The joy of right action."

57

FROM DELHI THE GURU PROCEEDED TO MATHRA, THE BIRTH place of Shri Krishna. the Lord of Yoga, the giver of Bhagwad Gita, the Bible of Hindu religion.

The Guru was in a mood of ecstasy as he entered the city; he walked to the river Jamna and the sight that met him grieved him greatly. The lanes and the banks of the river were crowded with mendicants who had abandoned their *Dharma* and now lived on alms. There on a heap of ashes a blind man lay grovelling. He was so emaciated that it was clear that he had gone without food for days ; he was mixing a handful of ashes in an earthen bowl to drink. The Guru's heart was touched with mercy. " Why are you drinking ashes ? " asked the Guru.

" I have been down with fever, " he answed. " I have not been able to go about and beg. I am starving; have pity upon me."

" Yes," said the Guru. He took a handful of water, uttered the name of God and sprinkled it on the eyes of the blind man.

Instantly the blind man got sight. He saw the Guru standing in front of him. He could not believe it. He thought he was dreaming and then suddenly realising the fact he fell at his feet.

" My dream has come true," he said. " I dreamed some days ago that a great teacher, Nanak, would come and give me sight. You are Nanak, God's messenger." He clung to the Guru's feet and washed them with tears of gratitude.

" I have done without eyes all my life and could do to the end, which cannot be far off. Give me the sight, O true teacher, to find the way to God."

The Guru smiled and said, " You shall have it." Then he showed him the way. He became the first Sikh of the Guru in Mathra. A crowd of men and women gathered round the Guru, as the news spread that a stranger had given slight to a blind man.

In an instant he was surrounded by a group of devotees, who were dancing, singing devotional songs and dancing, jumping, and going round in a circle. The Guru stopped and enquired, " What are they doing? "

" They are performing Kirtan," came the answer, " and are intoxicated with the love of God."

" The true devotees lose themselves in adoration of God and in a state of ecstasy may dance out of pure joy. They in whose heart the spark of devotion is covered with the dust of desire, merely jump about without the true impulse which moves the devotees of God. These men are merely play-acting without any overpowering joy of spirit."

The Guru turned to them and said, " The disciples play, the gurus dance, shake their feet and roll their heads, the dust that they raise falleth on their heads. The dancers dash themselves on the ground and others clap their hands and keep time, all this for the sake of earning food. The audience beholds their antics and laughs. Tell me, what spiritual and moral purpose do they serve ? "

Listen exclaimed the Guru:
" He is fearless and formless,
His name is true.
He who has created this universe.
To Him, the milkmaids sing.
The Krishnas sing,
Sita and royal Ramas sing.
They who with a mind thirsty with longing,
On nights full of unbroken calmness
Having received from the Guru the word
Acquire merit and receive the gift of right discrimination,
By Divine grace cross the ocean of life."

" Is there no meaning in the performance of these devotions ?" asked a simple villager.

" None," said the Guru. " Do oil presses, spinning wheels, handmills, potter's wheels, tops, churning staves threshing frames, birds whirling in the air and whirlwinds have any spiritual significance? So men have no significance who turn round round without the love of God. In life itself, innumerable men in unending streams turn the wheel of birth aud death, bound by the chain of their acts They dance their way to death. They who waste their days in laughter and dance will rue it, and weep when they depart. Learn that dancing and movements of the body are physical recreations and give no supernatural powers. Nanak says that those who have fear of God in their minds also conceive the love of God in their hearts."

The Guru walked on and came to a spot where the drama of Krishna and his Gopies was being staged. He stopped and watched the play. It symbolised Lord Krishna and his devotees in the form of a boy lover and the maids who loved him. The play had a meaning and spiritual value. The acting was good.

The Guru strode forward and said, "O ye men, see how Krishna's love reaches all his devotees. He the fearless, formless. Lord is one, while his devotees are numberless.

"There are many royal Ramas, many are the stories of
Krishna and many commentaries of the Vedas.
He chisels into form milkmaids,
To adore the cowherd Krishna,
Adorns him with scintillating jewels,
And makes sun and moon the curtain raisers.
The Lord is one
And all else is other than Him."

The crowd that had gathered round him begged him to teach them

"You are familiar with dancing in a circle and keeping time with the beating of the cymbals, but unless the body and mind are in tune with the infinite, the outer play-acting is of no avail. Listen," he said.

"Make wisdom the musical instrument
Longing for Him the accompanying drum,
This will awaken true desire,
And fill the mind with bliss.
This is ascetism, this is devotion,
Intoxicated with it dance with joy."

He continued following the same trend of thought pointing out how divine music could be made and salvation attained :

"Beat the drum,
With the hand of truth and contentment,
Tie bells of everlasting joy to thy feet,
In the sound of soundless sound,
Lose all sense of separation.
Imbued with this, dance step by step.
Any other dance is a physical performance,
Only he dances, who dances in perfect harmony of spirit.

A mind filled with the fear of the Lord,
Sitting and standing remembers Him,
Knowing that this body will turn to dust.

Advance imbued in this thought, step by step.
Only he dances, who dances in perfect harmony of spirit.

Treasure the true instruction
Given in the company of the good,
And the sacred name given by the Guru,
Nanak says again and again,
Imbued in this dance step by step,
Only he dances who dances in perfect harmony of spirit."

From Mathra the Guru proceeded to Brindaban followed by many people. He joined a crowd where the worshippers of Krishna had gathered.

A Sadhu approached the Guru, and enquired, "Do you not worship Krishna, the Lord of Vraj ?"

"I do not know him as the Lord of Vraj," said the Guru. "I only know the Lord of the Universe, who sustains the universe."

The Sadhu was overpowered by the truth and bowed in reverence.

The Guru said :
"There is one Krishna, God, the Lord of all gods.
He is the *atma-dev*, the God within all beings,
This *Atman* is all-pervading.
He who knows the secret commands my service.
He is beyond all illusion."

The Guru wandered into the forest of Brindaban where milkmaids and cowherds leaving all else followed the music of Krishna's flute. The Guru broke into divine melody and Mardana accompanied him :

"They who receive the call of love,
Like the *chakvi* pass the whole night,
Calling for their love, without a wink of sleep,
Longing for the unseen beloved,
Driven by the thirst of love.
Even a moment without Him is bereft of life for them.
The path of love is the gift of the beloved.

The lotus blows on the surface of water,
The sunbeam travels from the skies,
The fire of love that is kindled,
Mingles light with light.

The *chatrak* for a drop of rain,
Wails all day and night.
The rain pours in all regions.
Its thirst is not quenched
Without a rain-drop that reaches its lips.

The fish that is born and dwells in water,
Subject to pain and joy,

Cannot survive a minute without water,
Its living and dying depends on it.
She whose lover has gone to a far country
Receives the word from the true Guru,
Follows the path of virtue,
The lover dwells in her heart.
The spark of devotion thus kindled
The pain of parting is experienced no more.
With every breath she calls for the Beloved,
By the grace of the Guru she finds Him.
The Beloved is always with the lover,
By His grace the union is achieved.
The divine spark is in all,
It prevades every heart
By the grace of the Guru
He is revealed and the devotee enters the eternal calm.
He, the giver of peace, the Lord of all,
Perfects His own work Himself.
By the grace of the Guru, the Beloved is discovered within,
And the fire of life is quenched."

58

THE GURU THEN PROCEEDED TO AJMER AND VISITED PUSHKAR. He stood on the banks of the lake and saw crowds of men bathing in it. A Raja who thought he was bathing his sins and performing a great religious act looked at the Guru and saw him standing completely detached without any desire to bathe in the purifying *sagar*. He could not make out from his dress whether the Guru was a Hindu or a non-Hindu. He could not restrain himself and came to the Guru and said, " Why are you standing transfixed and not doing the right thing ? "

" What is the right thing ? " asked the Guru.

" To bathe in the *sagar*," said the Raja.

The Guru smiled and said, " Within you is the fathomless ocean of *gunas*. No one has fathomed its depth. Only by the grace of the Guru the immense, the limitless ocean, brimful of the waters of suffering can be crossed. The hunger of the desire cannot be appeased without the true name."

The Raja had been initiated by the priests into ceremonial religion and could not follow the Guru ; he was a seeker after truth. " Lift me out of this ocean of suffering," he pleaded.

" Brother," said the Guru, " The waves of pain keep the ocean of life in motion. We hug the waves of emotion, happy when we are tossed on the crest of the wave ; desperate when it drives us down into its depths. It is only in the light of the sacred name that we discover the secret of rising above the waves and submitting to His will, and following the calls of love and thus sterilise the seed of action. Listen :

You will have to render an account.
Don't be deluded by the glamour of the world.
In His court, only truth is accepted.
He who guards the gates of the mind
Accepts the harshness of life with resignation.
And waits like a mendicant and receives the alms of peace.
Nanak says his account is settled
Whose heart is kindled with devotion."

" I cannot follow you," said the Raja. " Speak to me in simple words.

" We sow the seed of Karma when, under the command of an asserting ego, we act for self-satisfaction, and reap the harvest of suffering. When we learn to submit to His will, we cease to make new Karma. We offer all our actions as a sacrifice and by a final act of self-surrender we remove the wall of separation and become one with Him."

" Ocean of compassion," said the Raja. " Lead me to the light and reveal to me the secret of worshipping God."

" The waves of desire set the mind wandering. There are three centres of sin, the mind, the body, and the tongue. The wafts of desire weave the chains of attachment. Attachment gives rise to aversion and thus misled by attachment and aversion man sinks deeper and deeper into the mire. When the sacred name enters the heart the desire for sense objects disappears, mind becomes calm like a pellucid lake and the path of salvation is seen."

" Which is the final *sadhan* to attain peace ? " asked the Raja. " How far are religious ceremonies, ordained by ancient scriptures, of help ? " The Guru said :

" Loud beats the drum of Vedas,
Its message is confused
By conflicting interpretations
Of various schools of thought.
Says Nanak, treasure the sacred name
Seek and find the truth."

" Rajaji," continued the Guru, " ceremonies however high-sounding and elaborate, do not kill the seed of desire, they only feed the desire that binds. The teachings of the Vedas and Shastras show not the way ; the great Pandits have coloured them with the colour of their own minds and formed various schools. Therefore, take shelter in the sacred word which is the basis of all Vedas. Surrender thyself to God and know the truth from thy own experience."

The Raja with his followers became Sikhs and the Guru after a short stay left the place.

59

THE GURU PROCEEDED TO UJJAIN. HE REACHED THERE ON THE full moon of the month of Kartik, at the time when a large gathering of pilgrims came to acquire merit by performing the pilgrimage of *avantika*.

They were lighting little lamps and floating them on the river in the hope of lighting the path of their dear ones who had departed.

The Guru watched them and then asked, " Why are you floating lamps on the river ? "

" Do you not know ? " said a priest. " That the way on the other side is dark and dreary and the little lights illumine the dreadful darkness of the road which the dead have to tread."

" Alas ! these lights are of no use," said the Guru. " I will tell you how to light the lamp to illumine the other side and to float it. Listen :

Make this body the float,
Light in it the lamp of realisation,
Transform the fire of desire into devotion.
Kindle with it the everlasting flame.
Merge consciousness with divine consciousness
Float such a lamp on the stream
Such a light illumines the darkness of mind
And awakens right understanding.

On the wheel of good actions mould the container.
A pure container becomes a receptacle of light.
Such light becomes a beacon light for all.
Such a light will not fail now or hereafter.
It is a rare seeker of truth who knows this secret.
By divine grace
In his heart such an unfailing light is lit
Which neither water can wet, nor the wind can blow out.
Enthroned in divine glory,
Its flame, untouched by the winds of desire
Guides the soul across the ocean of death.

Kshatry, Brahmin, Vaisha, Sudra,
Men belonging to a thousand and one castes
Can light this lamp
And cross the ocean of death."

A crowd gathered round the Guru and he continued, " My friends, just think. How can an earthen lamp shed its light on the other side, when the soul has left this body ? No material things go with it. It is the essence of its own actions, good and bad, that go with it, and only the light of all lights can light its path."

Many people begged him to stay and the Guru decided to stay with a poor untouchable. There was great consternation amongst the Pandits and the priests, and all those who were proud of their caste came and sat at a distance from the Guru.

" You are puzzled because I am staying with a good, kind and hard-working man, who is doing his duty," said the Guru. " Remember :

" He indeed is a Brahmin
Who sees Brahm in all,
Who is restrained and devoted to Brahm,
Who is established in calm content
Who has broken the bonds and attained ' MUKTI '—
Such a Brahmin is worthy of worship.
Actions determine caste,
Man exalts or lowers himself by his own acts.
By devotion to the sacred name
Release from the wheel of birth and death is obtained.
Do not worry about distinction of caste
Realise that His light is in all,
There is no caste on the other side."

Next morning the Guru sat on the river bank and a large crowd gathered round him, eager to hear him and learn the way of salvation.

" See yonder deep flowing stream its big, tossing waves break into drops and yet they are one with the stream," said the Guru. " He who knows this also knows His creation is in Him and his own self shares the essence of divine life: He who knows this is on the way of salvation. In the darkness of the night is hidden the light of the day. This mystery is not resolved without the guidance of the Guru.

" Man is in woman and woman in man ; sound dwells in the silence and meditation itself is in sound. This mystery cannot be unravelled ; those who unravel it are beyond the power of description. The light is in the mind, the mind partakes of light. O brothers, this is discovered by the grace of the Guru. They indeed are blessed whose consciousness is submerged in the sacred Name."

" The ruler of the place heard of the Guru. He was learned in the lore of established religion and came to see the Guru. He asked, " How did the world come into existence ? What is the disease of the mind and its cure ? "

" The world is the shadow of self ; destroy the self, and with it will disappear the shadow which obscures the light and then perchance you will perceive the ' how and wherefore ' of that which is beyond comprehension. The mind suffers from the obsession of selfhood, which burns with the fire of desire, when the mind is drawn back into the true self, the desire dies and with it all suffering ceases."

The Raja bowed. " Teach me how to subdue the mind, to discard the husks, and to meditate on truth." " Listen," said the Guru :

" The fire of desire is quenched by the waters of virtue.
Admission to His presence is impossible,
Unless desire for Him fills the heart.
If even for a moment He is forgotten,
The chronic disease of self disturbs the mind.
O man, every moment of thy life,
Dwell on the greatness of God :
They who never forget His name
Are rare on this earth.

Harmfulness and selfhood
And all doubts disappear,
When the true teacher is met,
Human consciousness mingles,
With divine consciousness,
And light with light."

The Raja asked, "How can this body be prepared for such a high destiny ?"

" By ceasing to be attached to that which must pass ; by clothing the body in garments of virtue to attract the Beloved. By the grace of the Guru, the bride that has become worthy is blessed by the bridegroom.

" Pour the water of the sacred name and quench the four fires of attachment, greed, anger and passion. The inner lotus will then bloom brimful with nectar. Seek the Guru, follow truth, and enter his realm."

60

THE GURU FROM UJJAIN TRAVELLED SLOWLY TO NASIK, where he took his seat on the banks of the Godavri. A banker approached him and offered him lodgings in his *dharamsala* which he had built for the comfort of pilgrims.

The Guru smiled and said, " The earth is my *dharamsala* and its canopy is the sky and I am waiting for my host."

The banker was still there when a poor goldsmith approached the Guru and humbly prayed, " Kind sir, will you bless my humble abode with your presence ? I can offer you nothing by way of comfort except my own humble services and my devotion."

The Guru turned to the banker. " See my host has arrived ! I was waiting for him." Thus saying he rose and followed the goldsmith to his house.

It was just a two-roomed hut with no furniture. They placed one room at the disposal of the Guru. The wife of the goldsmith brought water in an earthen jug, the goldsmith with great devotion washed the feet of the Guru and brought a plate of rice and dal and served the Guru and his companions. His every act was inspired with the spirit of service.

The banker who lived in a palatial building opposite the goldsmith's house walked in and saw the Guru lying down on the ground.

" You would have been more comfortable at my place," he remarked.

" How do you know I am less comfortable here ? " answered the Guru. " On those whom He denies the goods of the world He bestows His grace. He is the Giver of the needy. I stay with His favourites so that I too may receive His gifts. Learn ;

Desire for pleasure is the disease ;
Suffering its cure.
Peace enters the mind

When desire for pleasure exists no more.
When an individual ceases
To feel he is the doer
And knows that God is the doer,
He abides by His will
And enters the path of salvation."

The Seth walked away but the words of the Guru were ringing in his ears. Next morning as he proceeded to the river he heard Baba reciting :

" The whole world is in pain.
Says Nanak, only He is at peace
In whose heart dwells the name of God."

The banker was drawn to the Guru, but he could not bring himself to seek the Guru. The Guru knew what was passing in his mind. " I have a favour to ask you " he said, approaching the banker.

The banker was flattered. " My hospitality is at your service," he said.

" I want nothing," said the Guru, " but you are a banker and count your deposits in lakhs. Will you take this needle for me ; keep it and restore it to me in the next world."

The banker laughed, and said, " You are a simpleton ; we can carry nothing to the other side."

" Who is a simpleton, you or I ? You are gathering wealth which you cannot carry, while I am seeking that which can go with me."

" Come to my house," he begged, " and teach me the way of life."

The Guru agreed and walked with him to his house which was overflowing with servants. The banker led the Guru to his private apartments, brought a seat for him to sit and himself sat at the feet of the Guru.

" Tell me," he asked with folded hands, " the way of the peace. With all my possessions I have no peace. I am driven day and night on the path of misery. You are right ; the whole world is in pain."

" My brother," said the Guru sweetly, " just watch the processes which bring pain. The mind is filled with desire for things, this desire acts like a barb on the mind and drives the individual towards the attainment of the object of desire. When the desired object is attained, the anxiety to protect it allows no peace. Then when that which was purchased with such pain is lost, it leaves a deeper pain behind and lastly when death comes and all is left behind, it is the culmination of agony. There is no peace in things, which are subject to change ; change itself is the source of pain. Peace can only be found in Him, the unchanging. Devotion to Him through sacred name brings peace ; attachment to other things brings pain." The Guru then broke into a hymn :

" Great is thy glory, O Lord all-pervading,
Thy limit no one can know or describe.
Thou art in all beings, all beings are in Thee
Thy incalculable power permeates the universe.
Thou art the true Lord,

Whoever adores thee crosses the sea of life.
Nanak glorifies the Lord who acts
In the way He deems best."

The banker suddenly woke up from the state of ecstasy into which he had been thrown. He fell at the feet of the Guru.

" Save me, O great teacher," he asked. " Lift me out of the muddy waters of wordly wealth. Take me out of this morass and bless me with the gift of the sacred name. I ask of thee one more favour. Bless my wife with your presence. We had a son. He passed away and since his death my wife has been ill, unable to move from her bed. We have been devoted to each other and, though pressed on all sides, I have refused to marry again."

The Guru got up and followed the banker to the room of his wife, and she, as she saw the Guru entering, in her effort to rise and receive him, fell from the bed at the feet of the Guru. The Guru with his own hand raised her and in that raising she was restored to perfect health with the glow of youth. They were both astounded, fell at the feet of the Guru, and clasped them and touched them with their foreheads over and over again.

The Guru said, " Remember all that comes to being, must return to non-being ; all that you give is yours, all you keep is not yours. Make yourself a faithful servitor of the Divine Will and thus earn happiness here and hereafter. Make the scared word the sustenance of your lives."

The Guru then returned to the home of the goldsmith. The banker, from that day forward, gave all his money in charity and kept just enough for their own subsistence and out of this too he spent all that he could spare to help others.

The Guru left them, though they wanted to accompany him. He said the life of a householder was the best ; it was here that true renunciation could be practised and service rendered and the law of sacrifice observed.

61

THE GURU WENDED HIS WAY BACK TO DELHI AND WAS ABOUT to enter it when he saw a small crowd gathered round a man, who with upraised arms was delivering a lecture, upbraiding men for their lack of patriotism, their supineness and their spirit of subservience. The Guru joined the crowd, stopped and listened. He was amused at the gesticulations and assumed fervour of the lecturer.

" What is this idle talk ? " remarked the Guru.

The crowd turned towards him. " Why idle talk ? " asked several voices. " Our leader is speaking of serious things."

The Guru said, " It is a case of a fair show and a pretension of good actions, while he is moved by the eternal motive of selfishness. Let him deny, if he dares, that he was not planning to acquire new property and secure a higher status in society."

The lecturer was taken unawares and, in the Guru's presence, no one could utter untruth. He held down his head. " You are right, sir," he confessed.

" Learn," said the Guru :

" He who indulges in untruth
Feasts on carrion.
How can he teach others the truth
Who is deluded himself and deludes others ;
Such a leader only misleads."

After saying this the Guru walked on. He stopped in front of a palatial building, its gates were guarded on every side, by watchmen carrying swords and silver and gold maces. There was a display of wealth, of large possessions, overflowing treasuries and vast property. The Guru took his seat under a *pipal* tree, which was planted for worship by the owner just under the window of his bedroom. Some of the servants came and sat near the Guru. The Guru said :

" As we sow, so we reap.
Our deeds can earn riches or poverty.
Worldly wealth and its indulgence
Does not exalt the selfish enjoyer.
Earnest aspirations directed towards right and wrong
Make or mar a man's future."

The Guru then directed Mardana to tune his guitar, and sing the following hymn :

" You waste your night in sleep.
The day in feasting,
Precious time you barter away for shells,
You never remember God,
You will repent hereafter.
If your mind is bent on collecting wealth,
It is to earth you must return,
Again and again ;
You who make wealth your object,
Lose the real object of life.

If desire could secure its object.
Then all who desire would be rich.
The whole world is moved by desire :
It is deeds that bear fruit.
Sayeth Nanak, He who has created this universe
He sustains it also.
He is the giver of greatness :
Abide by His will."

The music of the guitar floated into the bedroom of the owner and the words of the hymn entered into his mind. Suddenly their meaning dawned on him and he realised it was a message for him. He hurriedly put on his clothes and hastened to the place where the Guru sat.

" Teach me, O master," he said.

" Learn," said the Guru. " We men depend on a signle life-breath and are given no time limit of living. O blind man dwell on this truth, life is uncertain. Remember him, Who is the Giver of breath and life. Life and body are His. He indeed is my Beloved. He is the true providence. If He does not bestow His gifts, how can there be any gain ? We get what our past actions can yield. Life is wasted in hypocritical actions. Without remembering God, driven to the gates of death, we repent for our deeds in the end."

" I have come to you," said the banker, " for your words reached and touched the innermost chords of my heart."

" It was not the grandeur of your house that attract me," said the Guru, " but the saving grace within you which has brought you to me. In the wordly success that has come to you, the final end must have escaped your notice. You must have thought that you can exploit the whole world, for your pleasure and benefit, regardless of the interests of others, trampling down rivals to conserve your own position. Your success is the result of your Karma in the past, but have you sown for the future ? Nothing that you have will go with you. The drums of death are beating. Prepare thyself for the journey."

" I will follow you," said the rich man. " Bless my house with your presence and enlighten my wives also."

" Wives ? " said the Guru. " Have you more than one ? "

" Yes," said the rich man holding down his head.

" Alas ! you wish to be loved by them all without knowing what love is yourself. Learn my friend, we can only love the one. They who scatter their affection in all directions know not the way of love. Like those who serve many gods, they fail to serve the one, with all their heart and with all their devotion."

" I have indeed erred," confessed the rich man.

" They who know they have erred and repent are forgiven," said the Guru.

The Guru then accompanied the rich man and entered his gorgeously furnished appartments and was soon surrounded by the ladies of the house.

The Guru then addressed them. " Listen," he said, " there are two paths, the path of self and the path of self-surrender. If we pursue the path of self, howsoever we strive for success, its achievement leaves behind only disappointment, and spurs the mind to further effort to the ultimate weariness of body and mind. The path of self-surrender bestows on the bride the love of the bridegroom and so, when we surrender ourselves to God, we open our heart for His love to enter and retrieve us from sin and sorrow. My friends, there is no other way ; submission to the divine will is the path of salvation ; assertion of self-will is the path of sorrow. The former offers immediate release, the latter subjection to our enemies ; passion, greed, delusion and pride.

They all bowed. " Tell us the way of righteous living," they all said.

"You, my brother," said the Guru, "should consider yourself a custodian of the wealth and use your powers so that the 'have-nots' may share the reward of your labours. He who earns and gives knows the way. The wealth that is hoarded has no real value, like gold that lies hidden in the depths of earth. Human use gives value to gold, so make your wealth of some use, for he who earns it knows how to spend it wisely and those who receive it know only how to squander it. You, my sisters, have the power to mould the future generation; dedicate yourselves to God and make yourselves the hand-maidens of the divine mercy and helpfulness. Then this house will be rich in true values and the love of all those who are helped will lighten its gloom."

After saying this the Guru came out and took his seat under the tree. A Muslim faqir came and asked the Guru, "What stands in the way of realising reality?"

"Desire for sense-objects," answered the Guru.

"What is the source of desire?" he asked. "I-am-ness," said the Guru.

"What do you mean by 'I-am-ness'?"

"The awareness of self apart from all else."

"How can this sense of awareness be removed?"

"By knowledge of self and its merging into God."

"How is this knowledge acquired?"

"The higher wisdom," said the Guru, "is clouded by the mists of wrong thinking and doing; when this clouding is removed by the neetar of the pure name, knowledge of self is the result."

"What is the sacred name?" asked the faqir.

"We all know," said the Guru, "the whole universe flowed from sound, the sound formed itself into the sacred name. The sacred name is the first manifestation of the unmanifest, in it all that is has its belng. It is the one word that leads the manifest to the unmanifest."

The faqir now shifted his ground. "Tell me the difference between a Hindu and a Muslim?"

"There is no real difference," said the Guru. "Hindus and Muslims are His. Their bodies are moulded in the same mould. Their spirit partakes of the same devine spark. The veil of ignorance only separates the two."

"What is this ignorance?" ask the faqir.

"Ignorance which prevents us seeing the truth. God is one, say the Muslims. If God is one, how can a Hindu be but a brother to a Muslim? But we do not worship God, we worship that which is untrue, and this worship of the unreal is the cause of separation and hate. When we approach God, all differences disappear."

"What is truth?" asked the faqir.

"God alone is true," said the Guru. "His name is true, he is all-pervading beyond fear and hate. Exalt His name and realise Him."

The faqir had come to expose the Guru, to defeat him in argument and now he found himself accepting him as his teacher.

62

THE GURU NOW RETURNED TO KARTARPUR. AFTER THE morning prayers were finished, the Guru sat in an open *diwan* and gave instruction. The disciples who gathered round the Guru brought their difficulties to him and sought a solution.

One morning a learned Sikh, who was well-versed in Hindu philosophy asked, " What is the origin of sin ? How can Jiva Atma sin, since it is divine in its essence ?

" There are many things which elude definition," said the Guru. " The roots of things are only known to Him who created this universe. For us it is enough to know that we commit sin, when to quench our thirst for things we temple on the rights of others. We must also know, that, trespass the law of love by our actions, we cannot escape the pain and punishment which is its inevitable consequence.

" All that is born is afflicted with the disease of egoism and is subject to the illusion of *Maya* and its suffering.

" The fever of self engenders the disease of acquisitiveness and it clouds the mind. From self again springs the fire of desire which is constantly fed by sense-objects."

" Who is the real performer of actions ? " the questioner asked again. " It cannot be the soul. How is the divine soul bound to the wheel of birth and death ? "

" Again," said the Guru, " the divinity of the soul is infinite and beyond the comprehension of human understanding. On the plane of action we know that hope and desire rule the mind, and action prompted by these makes bondage. The world is born of good and bad deeds. He who fails to take shelter in God is under their domain and is perishable."

" How does *Maya* enamour the mind," he asked, " and turn the divine soul into a slave ? "

" The dictates of the mind are translated into the will to act. It is the mind that conceives good and bad actions. Intoxicated with sense-objects, the mind never finds rest. It is satisfied and happy only when it turns to the true one."

" O Sat Guru, explain to us the mystery of dreams," asked another. " In a dream one sees without eyes. In a dream one hears without ears. In a dream the dead walk with the living. In a dream, time, nay even its makers, the sun and moon, do not seem to exist. In a dream future happenings are foreseen. What is it that makes dreams ? "

" What you say is true," said the Guru, " Dreams bear witness to the fact that sense organs are only vehicles used by the soul, on the physical plane, and that on a higher plane, the soul sees, hears, acts without its physical instruments and the barrier of time and physical death no more intervenes between the living and the dead. Past, present and future are transparent in a higher state.

" In sleep," continued the Guru, " day turns into unreality and on awakening the dreams vanish and become unreal. In sound sleep both this world and the dream world cease to exist ; consciousness is aware of itself. We dream when consciousness is a witness to outer impressions. We are awake when we are aware of the existence of world. When consciousness retires into itself beyond the bounds of waking and dreaming, nothing exists. In the foregoing states, consciousness acts within the three *gunas*, but in the fourth state, which is beyond the three *gunas*, it becomes one with the real. All things are within the three states. In the fourth state birth and death do not exist. There the pure light dwells which is the life of the world. It is made visible by the Guru by the power of soundless sound. Life and death are subject to the three *gunas*. The four books of knowledge explain this. They describe three states. The *turia* state, the Guru, the knower of God, alone can describe.

" Remember that all those who are born and die, as long as they are subject to the three *gunas*, are subject to change, pleasure and pain. It is only when the consciousness reaches the fourth state, *turia,* that the soul is established in its own self and the *Jiva Atman* becomes one with *Parmatman*."

" What are the three *gunas* ? " asked another.

" *Gunas* are aspects of energy : its manifestation in grosser form is Tamas, its active form is Rajas its pure form is Satva. It is Rajas in its active form which works for action, for progress, for achievement."

Then the Guru went into a state of ecstasy and sang the following hymn :

" This body is like an unbaked earthen vessel
It is made and unmade subject to suffering.
This world is an endless ocean,
It cannot be crossed without the favour of the Guru.
There is no other besides thee, my Beloved.

Thou art in all colours and forms,
He whom Thou favourest seeth thee.
Like a bad mother-in-law,
The darkness of ignorance prevents union with the Beloved.
I worship the feet of the friend,
Who has favoured me and removed the veil
And I have seen my Beloved.

Having subdued the mind by meditation
I find there is no friend other than Thyself,
Whether Thou sendest pleasure or pain,
I shall rejoice in Thy will.
In surrendering to thee, hope and desire have vanished,
The domination of the *gunas* is at an end.
Having taken shelter with Thee, Thy devotee,
With the favour of the Guru, has gained *turia* state.
Knowledge, recitation, meditation and austerities,
Are all accomplished when He, the infinite, fills the heart.
Nanak says, a mind that is imbued with the colour of His name
Under the instructions of the Guru, learns to serve the Lord.

63

THE GURU WAS HOLDING HIS DIWAN AS USUAL, WHEN A SIKH weeping bitterly fell at his feet and, almost stifled by sobs, managed to say, " I have lost my only son. I am ruined. O Sat Guru, my wife and I can find no peace. We find comfort in nothing."

The Guru lifted his head with his own hand from his feet. His mere touch almost cured the heart-ache of the bereaved parent.

" Brother, take courage," he said. " There is none in the world who has not suffered the loss of someone dear to him. The first to depart are those under whose loving care we grow from infancy to manhood and then one by one those go, whom we love and admire. The pain has its roots in pleasure. We suffer when that which gives us joy is taken away from us. They who are wise do not attach themselves to that which is passing. It is attachment to the impermanent and transitory which is the source of suffering. Everything in this world is in a state of flux. It is futile to associate intimately with that which must pass. Whosoever is born must go. Everyone has his turn. He, the Creator, is the only one permanently established ; all else comes and goes."

" Sat Guru," said another, " what is it that lives and never dies ? "

" That which is not subject to the three *gunas*," said the Guru, " and that which never floats and is not drowned. It is matter, which partakes of the three *gunas*, which changes the self which gives the life, is changeless. Remember he alone lives in whose heart He abides. None else is in reality alive. Now listen :

" The love of family is born of attachment to self.
Abandon attachment, it is replete with darkness,
O brother, wave off the delusion of attachment and doubt,
Receive the true name in your heart so that it becomes,
The life-breath of the body.

When the true name which is replete with nine treasures
Finds its way into the heart, there is no weeping for kith and kin.

In the ocean of attachment, born of ignorance, the world is drowning :
Only the righteous cross this ocean.
This attachment binds us to the wheel of birth.
This attachment again leads to the realm of death.

Receive instructions from the teacher and escape the noose of the net of death—

Unless attachment vanishes, the bonds are not broken.

By His grace attachment vanishes
And the disciple becomes one with God."

The disciple bowed and asked again, " Why is this *Jiva* born and why does it die again and again ? "

" The *Jiva* inspired by the will to live, persists in affirming the self, aware of its own individuality," said the Guru. " In self-assertion this world exists, self-assertion is the bondage created by the self itself. Self-assertion is the disease, self-surrender the cure. The asserting self performs acts, for the satisfaction of the self, and thus builds its own character, which determines its present and its future."

" In the hope of living, the world works for its own death. The hope never dies and there is no escape from birth and death. Hope finds fulfilment when he seek the feet of God."

A Sikh who had just come, stopped for a short while and then rose to go.

" Why are you in such a hurry to depart ? " enquired the Guru.

" Sat Guru," he said, " I am in attendance on a friend who is very ill and altogether helpless. There is no one to look after him. He was feeling worse when I left him this morning, but I could not miss my daily sight of you."

" It is more important to follow my instructions than to come to see me, said the Guru. " You have ignored my teaching by coming to me to serve yourself, instead of serving him whom God has placed in your care."

" Forgive me," said the Sikh, " O Sat Guru, I have indeed erred and neglected my duty. I came to you to gratify the self."

" Remember," said the Guru, " that it is more important to follow what I teach than to see me. Your duty was with the patient."

The Sikh fell at the feet of the Guru, begged his forgiveness and departed.

" See," said the Guru, when the Sikh was gone, " how self intrudes upon men of good intentions. Indeed until the individual self melts into God-consciousness, there is no freedom from desire, from self-expression and from gratification of the self. Separation is the life-breath of the ego, and it does all it can to strengthen the will to separate. As we turn towards God, his compassion for all creation enters our hearts and as this feeling to serve our fellow-men increases, the sense of separation decreases and *Jiva* moves to be one with its source. Listen :

> The light of dawn breaks forth, when the ego dies.
> Then the tide of good-will for all fills the heart.
> He who sees himself in all that exists,
> He indeed is exalted, says Nanak."

The Guru continued, " Such a one becomes one with God and becomes responsive to joy and sorrow which sweep this whole creation."

Salis Rai, the jeweller, who had been listening with rapt attention, then asked, " Tell me how to find the way to happiness in this world ? "

" They alone can find the way of happiness, said the Guru, " who know the truth. They are happy in the four worlds. Having subdued the ego, and with it the thirst for things, they are absorbed in truth."

" What happens to those, " he asked, " who do not realise the truth ? "

" He who does not realise the truth, " said the Guru, " burns in the fire of desire, but he who knows his own self, becomes one with the infinite God. "

" What are the characteristics of a good man ? " asked the jeweller.

" A good man, " said the Guru, " does not wrap himself in indifference. He returns good for evil, his heart is empty of hate and envy. He suffers when others suffer. He is happy when others are happy, while a man who is not good hates others, is indifferent to the suffering of others, and cannot bear to see any one prosper."

" What are the characteristics of a devotee ? " asked a Sikh.

" A devotee, " said the Guru, " is like a virgin bride, who surrenders herself to the bridegroom without any thought of self. A devotee is no more aware of his separate self in the service of the Beloved. The image of the Beloved fills his heart till all sense of separateness departs and the devotee becomes one with the object of devotion. "

" Tell me, O great teacher, how should a householder live ? "

" Listen, " said the Guru, " he who earns his living by hard labour and shares it with others, he follows the true path. "

" What should be the characteristics of your Sikh ? " asked Bhagirath.

" He who is truthful, contented and compassionate towards all, he who is free from covetousness and hate, he who is harmless, dispassionate and desireless, he who is self-controlled and has learnt to discriminate between right and wrong, he who surrenders himself to the supreme God and learns to abide by His will, such a harmonised person has entered the path of discipleship. "

64

ONE DAY MANI LAL ASKED THE GURU, " YOU SAY THAT THE sacred word has the power to transmute suffering into bliss, egoism into selflessness, but how is the sacred word to possess the mind ? My effort to repeat the sacred word never reaches the heart of my being. "

" It is only when we win His favour by righteous living, that we acquire the power to repeat the sacred name. It is then that the word reaches *Jiva Atma* and lifts it to *Parmatma*. Then the *Jiva Atma* and *Parmatma* become one and duality is destroyed. It is only through the grace of the Guru that this is known and the domain of death is left behind. "

" It sounds so easy, " said Mani Lal, " when you speak, O sat Guru, but the veil of darkness persists and refuses to be lifted. "

" When we practise truth, " said the Guru, " His light illuminates the darkness of the mind and it no more clings to this poisonous world. Living the life of a householder, a devotee, by the Guru's grace secures salvation."

" Forgive me, O Sat Guru, but how can I practise truth and be worthy of the grace of the Guru ? "

" It is by serving Him that we follow the path of the truth, and by surrendering to him what is His. Such service pleases the Master and, when accepted by Him, He bestows His grace."

" It is not easy to be attached to the invisible. " said Mani Lal. " It is still more difficult to know how to serve Him, when no direct service can be rendered. "

" To love His creation is to serve Him, " said the Guru. " Instal the image of the Guru in your heart, then you will get all that you desire. The true Lord with His grace accepts such a servant and removes the fear of death from his mind. "

" How should one begin to transfer the mind from worldly activities to divine activities ? "

" You must begin, " said the Guru, " to meditate on truth and cultivate devotion to the true word. The fruit of recitation and austerities is hidden in the true word ; it leads you to the door of salvation. "

" Sat Guru," said another Sikh, " you once said that this mind sometimes scales the skies and at other times sinks to the lower regions. This greedy mind is never stable. It wanders in every direction. "

" I am glad you have asked the question, " said the Guru. " Without the control of the mind the object is never attained. A mind under the cloud of passions cannot reflect the light of truth. It is only when clouds disperse, under the directions of the Guru, that it turns to Him again. The pure *Atma* has come under the sway of the *gunas*. It is by His grace that it is released from their sway. "

" How does it pass under the sway of the *gunas* " enquired the Sikh.

" This is a mystery which is not easy to explain, " said the Guru. " Words can only describe objects that we know and what is not known, no word can describe. Know this that creation exists under the interaction of the three *gunas* and freedom is gained when their sway is over. The spirit in the State of evolution wanders in search of the objects of desire and becomes captive by the creation of its own *Karma*. In turning away from the objects of senses and in turning to God it finds release again and becomes one with Him. "

"Having entered the plane of *Maya*, " the Guru continued, " we are lost in pursuit of illusions of the *Maya* and find no rest. It is only by invoking His name that we find the path of salvation. "

" Men gamble away their lives, " continued the Guru, " for the sake of a wife, sons, elephants and houses and gold. This is not the way to attain control over one's mind, which is the key of liberation. "

" They who gather the wealth of the world, their minds never find rest. Pleasure and pain become their door-keepers. They can gain peace only when they turn to God. When, by divine favour, the seeker meets the true teacher and under his directions gives up vices and acquires virtues, he then receives the gift of the word. There is no freedom from misery without the power of the name. They who are unrighteous cannot escape from the snare of *Maya* ; only by a good *Karma*, a person becomes righteous and receives the gift of knowledgo. The fickle wandering mind then becomes attached to the reality and is no more fascinated by the filth of the world. Such a person, says Nanak, chants praises of God."

" You, O divine Guru, say that everyone is engulfed in hope and fear," said another, " and infected with the virus of passion and wrath, hunger and thirst ; only a rare one is free from these. Tell us, O Sat Guru, how to gain freedom ? "

" The mind is in the body. Pour into it acts of truth. When truth enters the mind, the mind is transmuted into an image of truth."

The Guru continued, " It is only by continuous struggle that desire is driven out of the mind, then the source of life is discovered and the mind finds peace in the innermost recesses of the heart. He alone knows the essence, who knows the self. This is possible only when the five enemies are destroyed, and the true one enters the mind. An unrighteous person can never discover the key of salvation. It is only He who performs pure deeds who is fit to receive the word of God."

65

ONE DAY A PANDIT CAME AND AFTER ATTENDING THE morning prayers asked the Guru, " Can you tell us how this world came into existence ? "

" How strange," said the Guru, " that we know nothing about our own coming on this earth and we want to know how the whole creation came into being. You want to know at what time, at what epoch, at what lunar day and day of the week, in what month in what season the world was created. If the Pandits had known this they would have recorded it in the Puranas, if the Prophet had known it, He would have recorded it in the Quran. No one knows anything about it. Only the Creator who fashioned the world knows it." Then the Guru closed his eyes and uttered the following hymn :

" For unlimited period there was darkness. There was neither heaven nor earth, there was only the boundless word. There was neither sun nor moon, neither day nor light, He alone was in a state of *Samadhi*. There were no species nor speech, neither air nor water. No creation nor its dissolution nor birth nor death. Neither there were divisions of the earth, nor the seven regions ; neither were there oceans nor rivers nor was there water flowing.

" There existed neither the Vedas, nor other sacred books, neither the Puranas nor the Smritis. There was no reading of the Puranas. Nor was there any sunrise or sunset. There was nothing else except Himself. He was the speaker and listener. He Himself recognised Himself, the Unknowable. When it pleased Him he created the world, and made it exist without any support."

66

A BRAHMIN WHO HAD SOME PRETENCE OF LEARNING THEN asked, " What binds the soul of man to the wheel of birth and death ? What is the cause of pleasure and pain ? "

" Both pleasure and pain are the fruit of past actions. Man can blame no other but himself. His deeds, good and bad, bring pleasure or pain. The origin of Karma is only known to Him whose law prevails. This, however, is true. Man comes to earth with the sense of 'I-am-ness' fully developed, resolved to live for self, bound in the chains of hope and desire. He brews poison and with it poisons his own life and that of others."

"How can a man rid himself of the bondage of action and of the poison of his own brewing ?"

"He who purifies himself in the sacred pool of truth and adores God, praises Him, fills his consciousness with real love, God manifests Himself in his heart and makes him one with Him. He no more remains entangled in the noose of death. They who :

Day and night wish ill to others,
And never remember God,
They are doomed to be victims of the womb
They come and go, are born and die."

"The heart does not throb with love ; consciousness refuses to be one-pointed," said a seeker. "How can an aspirant harness these two recalcitrants in the cause of salvation ?"

"Gultivate contentment, truthfulness and forgiveness," said the Guru. "O Brother, the Giver of gifts bestow the power. Seek the shelter of the true teacher, know the self and, from knowing the self, acquire the knowledge of the universal self. The unrighteous are drowned in untruth and deceit."

"Teach us, O Guru, how to know this self ?

"Five elements make the body, In it also dwells the jewel of God," said the Guru. "Realise it. The *Jiva* is of God, one with God, and by concentration on the word it reveals itself."

"Tell us more," asked several voices.

"Listen," said the Guru,

"Body makes the paper, mind the ink,
Good and bad deeds make the writing.
Past actions produce our present acts,
Wondrous are the ways of God.
In the mad pursuit of the world
Why dost thou not remember Him ?
In forgetting Him, all virtues depart.

Every hour makes a mesh of the net,
In the snare of night and day
Thou eagerly seekest enjoyment, O simpleton.
And get more and more enmeshed in the net.

The body is like a furnace,
Mind like an iron under five fires.
The charcoal of sin feeds the fires,
And the mind knows no peace.

It burns and gets distorted.
Only Guru's word can transmute it,
Into pure gold by imparting the sacred word,
And dower it with peace."

67

AT KARTARPUR A LARGE NUMBER OF DISCIPLES GATHERED round the Guru. He started a regular devotional service. The Guru rose before dawn and had his bath, and so did the disciples. Before dawn Japji and Asa-di-War were recited and followed by the singing and expounding of hymns. The day was started with heart full of God. In the evening Rahras was recited, followed by singing of Arti, and at bedtime the Sohilla was sung. Thus morning, noon and night the disciples of the Guru were instructed to live in the light of true teachings.

There was a boy of about seven years of age, who regularly attended the early morning service and never missed any congregational prayer.

"My son," the Guru asked him one day, "what brings you here ? At your age boys sleep till late in the morning and pass their days in play."

The boy bowed to the Guru with folded hands and touched his feet. " It is you who call me here," he said. " One day my mother asked me to light a fire. I found that little sticks caught the fire before the thick ones were ignited, so I thought any day my turn may come and I decided to prepare myself for the journey."

"You speak like an old man and you indeed are wise. I call you Bhai Budha. You are right. Life is like a flowing stream that appears and disappears in hills and valleys. It is well to be prepared and to fill the mind with one colour only : that is His colour."

The Guru then uttered the following hymn :

"A fish swimming in deep water,
Wise and beautiful and all too trusting
Does not realise that it may fall in fisherman's net :
Tempted by desire it walks into the noose of death.
Brother realise that death is lurking at the corner.
Just like a fish, man is caught in the noose of death.

The whole world is subject to a time limit.
Only the Guru is beyond its limit.
They who are imbued with truth are freed.
The thieves and evil-ones are bound.
Blessed are they who stand at His door
Resplendent in the garments of truth.

Like birds in the net held by a bird-catcher,
Only he whom the Guru helps is saved,
The rest picking their food, are lost :
No other help is available except that of His name.

Dwell on the true one, He is enthroned in truth.
They who live in truth, their minds find rest in truth,
They indeed are pure, who have this knowledge.

Pray to the Guru to take you to the Beloved.
True happiness is gained when the Beloved is met.
The myrmidon of death shall trouble you no more :
When the sound of the word fills the mind.

The darkness of mind is not removed without the Guru.
Without the word, there is no awakening.
The Guru reveals the invisible
Awakens the love of truth
And shows the way to cross the domain of time—
And mingles light with light.

Thou art the friend, thou art the knower,
Thou also the guide who unites.
Blessed is the true teacher whose goodness knows no limit,
Death cannot reach where the Guru's word prevails.
Under His command all come forth.

Under His command they perform acts.
Under His command they remain subject to time.
Under His command they are absorbed in reality
Nanak says, these creatures have no power
They act as He commands."

One of the audience then rose and asked, " If we act under His command, have we no free will of our own ? Without it how can we seek salvation ? "

" Have I not already said that God's name has the power of liberation and of releasing the seeker from the bondage of acts which bind, but it is again by His grace that this secret is discovered. Our acts are determined as long as ' I-am-ness ' rules, but when we free ourselves from ' I-am-ness,' we exercise free will."

" How are the soul and body bound together ? " asked another.

" The three *gunas* make this body and he who comes to being is under their sway."

" How is one freed from their domination ?" asked another.

" As essence mingles with essence, as metal when melted becomes one with metal, so he who learns to love the Lord becomes one with the Beloved."

The boy devotee from that day was known as Bhai Budha and was much respected by the Guru himself and his successors. He was held in such esteem that he was given the privilige of conferring Guruship on five successors of Guru Nanak.

A PARTY OF SADHUS CAME TO KARTARPUR. THE GURU received them with great cordiality and they prolonged their stay with the Guru. The leader of the party was greatly impressed. He was a seeker after truth and approached the Guru and asked him to show the way.

" The weak and the wavering cannot follow the way,'' observed the Guru. " We must gain inner strength so that the impermanent and changing acquires no hold on the mind. Actions performed to serve the self, create *karma* which has to be fulfilled. The desire for self-satisfaction nurses the roots of suffering, in desiring pleasure, we reap the harvest of pain. When by right action this desire is extinguished, then we get spiritually strong and take the path of salvation, which is shown to those who are prepared to take it. This world is a passing show of four days. We search what is pleasant and avoid what is unpleasant. They who talk are many, but in their search for the sweets of life they swarm and die like flies. Only a rare one knows the meaning of renunciation.''

The leader of the Sadhus bowed and asked, " What you say is true, O Guru, tell me more about it."

" With great travail we gather things of the world," said the Guru, " Great is our suffering when we part with them. The fire of hunger is not appeased by feeding it with fresh fuel. The more it is fed, the more flames it creates. The demands of the body for enjoyment of dainties are equalled by the suffering they cause."

" You are a true teacher," said the leader. " I became a mendicant in search of peace and failed to find it. I am still a slave to the five passions of the body. Have mercy on me. Lead me to the light of all lights ; the abode of eternal peace.''

" Listen,'' said the Guru :

" This body is the temple of the Lord,
In it dwells the infinite light.
By the grace of the Guru a disciple is called
To enter the inner temple to be united with Him.

By renouncing adultery,
And desire for other people's wealth and the poison of selfhood,
Malice, jealousy, backbiting, covetousness and pride,
This temple is made pure.

Then the infinite, the boundless,
Seated in the temple
Receives from Him the nectar,
On him the Guru bestows the jewel of the word.

He treats pleasure and pain as the same,
The good and bad of the world undisturbed
He loves the company of His devotees
And by the practice of the sacred word attains true wisdom.

The Guru gives the sacred word
Moved by divine compassion,
Only he receives it who wins His favour
He bestows his gifts and the devotee gathers the treasures."

The leader of the party was so impressed that he became a disciple of the Guru, and his followers followed him.

69

" SIR, YOU ALWAYS SAY THAT A GURMUKH IS EXALTED AND A Manmukh remains bankrupt. Teach us how to distinguish between the two," asked a disciple.

" He is holy, he is righteous, he is Gurmukh who is sympathetic and happy in the happiness of others."

" How are they known, O Guru," asked Kala.

" By their actions," said the Guru. " A good man is pleased at hearing the praises of others ; he serves the poor and the needy. He shows honour and respect to the virtuous and the learned and all those who follow the way. He avoids subjects of discussions which give rise to quarrels. He serves those who are superior to him in intelligence or devotion. He uses his power, not arrogantly in trampling the rights of others but in protecting them. His pure intentions find expression in daily actions, such as faithfulness to his wife and respect for all other women, avoidance of evil company, and seeking the society of holy men as a result of good living, the craving for God's name grows in intensity and he cannot find rest without God's name."

Bhagat and Ohri asked, " How can one became a Gurmukh ? "

The Guru said, " By avoiding Manmukh Karma (evil acts)."

" What is Manmukh Karma ? " they asked.

" Know him to be a Manmukh who is envious of everyone and who regards all men as his enemies and hates them ; who desires that worldly wealth and all happiness should desert others and come to him. He suffers great pain when he beholds the houses, property and possessions of others.

" He who follows the Guru's instructions is Gurmukh and who turns away his face from them and follows the impulses of his own mind is Manmukh. A Manmukh is relentless and proud. He laugheth at persons inferior to him, treateth them with contempt, and glorieth in his own intelligence. A Manmukh is addicted to slander. If anyone praises another who is superior to him Manmukh cannot endure it and exclaims, ' Oh, I know him well he is not what he appears to be !' He obstinately follows the impulses of his selfish mind. All his actions express envy, pride, slander and obstinacy.

" He who is conceited, who is envious, cannot follow the path of the Guru.

" They who turn to the Guru drop these tendencies as trees drop their leaves in autumn and wear their new garments in spring."

70

MAKHDOOM PIR BAHA-UD-DIN'S SUCCESSOR HAD MET THE GURU in Multan. Now that he felt that his journey on earth was drawing to a close he came to see the Guru. The Guru welcomed him. He said, " My boat is now loaded and ready to take to the unknown seas. Can you help me to lighten the load ?

" My friend," said the Guru, " we carry the sack which we have sedulously filled, but the grace of His mercy can lighten the load of those who empty their heart of self and stand at His door for forgiveness."

The Pir sat silent, lost in deep meditation.

" I also feel," said the Guru, " that I have fulfilled my mission and must return home. I feel happy that the day is drawing near."

71

THE GURU RETURNED TO KARTARPUR AND TOOK HIS ABODE there. One morning just at the time of sunrise, he walked to the river Ravi which flowed close by. Some of his disciples followed him. They were walking in the sun behind them.

One of the disciples moved forward, bowed and asked the Guru, " How is it that we cannot dispel the illusions of the Maya ? "

" Just look at the shadows," said the Guru. " You can travel miles and miles and your shadows will precede you so long as the sun is at your back. Now turn your faces towards the sun, where are the shadows ? "

" They have disappeared," they said. " They are left behind."

" Learn this," said the Guru, " as long as our faces are turned away from God, the shadows of Maya hold us, but as soon as you turn your faces towards God, the shadows disappear."

" What prevents our turning to God," they asked.

" A man is born, because in him there is desire to become. Driven by desire, he lives and enjoys the fruits of the earth, at death he carries the seed which his actions fed, and is bound by it. He reaps in suffering the fruit of his wrong doings. It is only when he follows the right path as instructed by the Guru, that he secures his release by the power of the sacred name."

" It is not easy to follow the right path," said several disciples. " How should one prepare for the journey's end ? "

" Seek the company of men in whose mind God dwells. Listen to what they say, sing the praises of God and in doing so surrender thy will to the divine will. Under such a discipline, the wandering mind will cease to pursue sense-objects ; it will find satisfaction in dwelling on God and turn from the unreal to the real."

" You say, sir, that we should perform the duties of the household. How can these be performed without concentrating the mind on their performance ? "

" I can explain to you but you will not understand until your mind turns towards God. When that happens, your heart will be with the Beloved, and your hands will perform the acts. The mind that is God-filled is only conscious of Him and unconscious of all else. All acts are then performed under the light of Divine Command."

" How should a devotee live ?" asked a Sikh.

" Look at yonder river, flowing without pause, under the command of the law. Let your life flow as the river under Divine command, submit thyself to the Divine will, as an elephant submits to the ankus of the driver, as an anvil submits to the hammering of the blacksmith, always placing its head before the hammer. Thus place your body and mind at the service of the Lord and serve Him through pain and suffering. Thus we gain the key to the closed door."

" Why is it that Satnam, the true name, precedes all hymns ? " asked a disciple.

" Some propitiate Durga, some propitiate Shiva, some Ganesh and some other gods, but Sikhs worship only one God whose name is true. His name is above all that exists in all the worlds. Therefore, we seek his protection by invoking His name at the beginning of all hymns."

One day a Sikh approached the Guru with folded hands. " Sat Guru, Hindus and Muslims follow laws given by their law-givers and the prophets. What law must we follow ? "

" The law of truth," said the Guru. " Falsehood fades away but the truth prevails."

" How is it that every action arouses a feeling of uncertainty and consequently fear."

" All actions are performed in a threefold manner ; first desire arises in the mind, secondly it finds expression in speech and thirdly it impels the organs of action to act. All actions are performed to meet the demands of desire, and consequently are shadowed by anxiety and fear, lest failure may haunt the effort instead of success.

The fear of losing what has been acquired fills the mind with unceasing anxiety."

72

THERE LIVED IN A VILLAGE KHADUR LEHNA, A GREAT devotee of the goddess Jawala-Mukhi, the goddess of the flaming mouth. He worshipped the goddess of flame with pure and sincere devotion, and visited her temple near Kangra twice a year, walking full of devotion to offer his humble savings at her feet. He often met one Jodha, who also lived in the same village and heard from Jodha the hymns of Guru Nanak. Lehna was much impressed by what Jodha told him about the Satguru, and begged Jodha to take him to the Guru. Jodha readily agreed and they both came together to Kartarpur and joined the crowd that had gathered round the Guru. They attended the morning prayer, and listened to the praises of God sung by the choir. For a few days Lehna quietly listened to the sermons delivered by the Guru. Lehna was much impressed and deeply stirred by the prayers sung and the inner chords of his heart were touched. He immediately discarded the thread he wore round his neck as a sign of belonging to the cult of the goddess, and he came forward and fell at the feet of the Guru.

" Accept me, O great teacher," he pleaded.

The Guru lifted him with his own hands, and said, " I have been waiting for your coming. What is your name ? "

" My name is Lehna" (which means the receiver).

The Master smiled and said, " You are indeed a receiver, you have to take what I owe you."

The Guru embraced Lehna, and, in that embrace, endowed him with light.

" You have now become one with me, and henceforth you will be known as Angad—one with me in body and soul."

One day a Yogi who practised control of his breath came to the Guru and asked : " O great teacher, tell me how it is that inspite of my performing prolonged Pranayamas, my mind can never gain tranquillity. It wanders even in the process of my meditation and afterwards entirely without control."

" The answer is simple," said the Guru. " You wish to control the mind by control of breath, which is a physical process, and the mind is superphysical and therefore it is beyond the control of mere physical action. Till mind itself is washed clean, it can never be tranquil. When mind becomes tranquil breathing is automatically stopped."

" They say," said the Yogi, " that there are *nadees* (hidden streams) of power within this body, and that by the inhalation and exhalation of breath, these can be stirred and the control of breath subdues the usual activities of the mind, as it becomes motionless with the stopping of breath. In Hatha Yoga the right nostril, Ida, is the vehicle of the sun, the left side Pingla, that of moon. The breath inhaled through the right nostril partakes of the sun, is retained in Sushmana, the central stream which is called Brahmnadi, and is exhaled through Ida. The retaining of breath in Sushmna awakens the hidden powers of Kundalini."

" My dear friend," said the Guru, " you are well-versed in the system of Hatha Yoga. You have also practised and discovered that these outer restraints cannot awaken the soul and secure salvation. You may acquire superphysical powers, but they perish with the body. It is not by drawing on the sun or the moon, but by drawing up the sun—that is, by overcoming the energy from which springs actions, and by nourishing the moon, the spirit of mellow tranquillity, that the vagrant mind, which wanders like the wind and is restless like a fish, is brought under control. By controlling the motive power, the consciousness can no longer fly and dart in all directions but abides in the inner temple, protected by ramparts of virtue. The mind is endowed with three qualities Sat, Raj and Tamas ; it remains inert when Tamas dominates, under the influence of Rajas it become active, and it becomes tranquil when Satva prevails."

" How can one throw off the domination of Tamas and Rajas ? " enquired the Yogi.

" O ignorant Yogi," said the Guru, " why don't you take shelter in Him, who is supreme bliss ? In the fire of His love burn away that which is otherwise incombustible, the ego, take hold of the wandering mind and let its activities die. When you acquire the gift of faith, you will drink nectar and attain Samadhi. He whose mind is filled with God, drinks nectar and attains Samadhi. He whose mind is filled with God drinks nectar with every breath."

" It is not true that these Gunas dominate man ? " asked the Yogi.

" Yes," said the Guru. " The Gunas are aspects of the creative impulse which makes the world. Tamas makes for material stability, Rajas for progress and Satva for return of the pure to the pure. Rajas stirs up action and awakens thirst for things. If Rajas dries up, the self is realised and the mind becomes one with God and reality is realised.

" Youth, wealth and flowers
Fade away like fleeting days ;
Like autumn leaves that fall,
Falling to be renewed in spirit.
Revel in the joy of life,
In the springtide of youth.
In a few days this garment of the body will be weary.
My joyful friends are gone
To sleep in the dreary land of the dead.
I weep with drooping head
Like the lamenting bards.
Has thou fair maiden
Failed to hear the truth ?
Thou too must leave thy home
And go to thy bridegroom's home.
Thou sleepeth heedless
While the thieves are busy
Stealing thy stock of good deeds,
Leaving only misdeeds behind."

73

ONE DAY THE DISCIPLES OF SHEIKH BEHRAM, WHO WAS devoted to the Guru, came to see him. They had been asking many questions of the Sheikh who told them to go to Guru Nanak who would answer their questions.

" Tell us something of the Beloved," asked the leader of the party.

" Listen," said the Guru :
" The Beloved himself is the enjoyer,
Himself the essence of the enjoyment,
Himself appears in bridal robes
Himself the bridegroom of the bridal bed.
My Lord and Master is resplendent,
In His glory.
He pervades all things.

He Himself is the flowing water,
Himself the fisherman,
Himself the net,
Himself the fisherman's hook
Himself the fish, Himself the hidden ruby.
O my friends, in an infinite variety of colours
Appears my Beloved
He meets His devotee daily
May He have compassion on us.
Praise Him, He is the lake
He is the swan, He is the lotus in bud,
Himself the lotus in bloom
Its witness and its enjoyer."

Angad bowed and asked, " Satguru, why are some accepted and some not accepted ? "

" Close your eyes and look within," said the Guru. " Words are useless, experience affords true revelation."

Angad obeyed and when he opened his eyes he was full of gladness.

The Pir of the Sufees asked, " What has made you happy ? "

" I cannot tell," said Angad, " Hama Ost (He is all in all)."

" Listen," said the Guru :

" He alone who tastes this delicacy knows its taste. He cannot tell just as a dumb man cannot describe the taste of the sweets he enjoys. What can one say about Him, who cannot be described ? All that is given to us is to abide by His will and thus become harmonised."

" Tell us more," asked another. " How can we appear with shining faces before Him ? "

" He appears with a shining face, whose self dies while living, who destroys the ego, who breaks his bonds and whose thirst for things is quenched. The sacred word dwells in all beings, but only rare true seekers discover it."

" How can we discover it," asked several voices.

" Five evils are embedded in the innermost recesses of the mind. These give it no rest and the mind wanders ceaselessly."

" How do they effect the mind ? " asked another.

" These five enemies generate thirst for things. Desire burns like a fire and like thirst or hunger is never wholly satisfied."

" How can its fire be quenched ? "

" The fire of desire can only be extinguished by the sacred word. First we must begin a struggle with the mind, subdue these five enemies, then the desire vanishes and the mirror of the mind is ready to reflect His light. The one thing needful is to control the mind and to prevent its wandering."

" But this mind eludes control," said the questioner.

" Yes," said the Guru. " But till the mind is subdued the light does not shine in it. With the conquering of the mind the whole universe is conquered."

The Guru continued, " A novice must begin by exercising control over the mind by continuous watchfulness over thoughts when these are brought under control and there will arise the power of discrimination between the good and the bad, the changing, and unchanging, the real and unreal. It is only thus true knowledge is gained and not by cleverness of the mind.

" Listen," said the Guru :

" The immortal bird that can discriminate
Between milk and water, good and bad
Finds joy at the lake of knowledge
Which is brimful with rare pearls
On which the immortal bird feeds.
The heron and the wise crow,
They never discover this lake
For their food is not in it.
What they need is quite different.
They who work for truth attain truth
They who work for untruth remain in untruth.
They who receive His commands from above
Meet the Satguru."

74

A PARTY OF SIDHAS, THOSE WHO HAD ACQUIRED CERTAIN superphysical powers, came to Katarpur and wanted to test the Guru. They invited the Guru to attend a fair at Achala, where they were going, knowing that it would be impossible for the Guru to reach there on the date given. The Guru readily accepted the invitation.

The Sidhas departed, full of amusement that the Guru could never reach the place. They were surprised when on arrival they found the Guru seated under a tree. A non-Sadhu had beaten them at their own game. They immediately started a discussion with him.

" Can a householder acquire powers and reach God ? " asked Gopi Nath.

" Yes," said the Guru, " a householder who controls himself, who makes self-restraint and meditation his daily sustenance, who makes his body a vehicle of giving,

" He is as pure as the water of the Ganges
Such a householder becomes the incarnation of the truth
The supreme essence is formless and undivided."

" Then what about the *Abdhoot*, who renounces all things ? "

" The *Abdhoot* who burns his self
And makes penance his sustenance

And stands for alms in the city of the heart
Such an *Abdhoot* ascends to the city of Shiva.
Such an *Abdhoot* becomes an incarnation of truth."
The supreme essence is formless and undivided."

"What about him," asked Gopi Nath, "who has become an *Udasi* and has lost all interest in the world ?"

He indeed is an *Udasi* who nurses his *Udas.*
Unaffected by pleasure or pain who dwells in the Lord.
Unites the sun and the moon,
Such an *Udasi* is no more affected
He becomes one with the essence
The supreme essence is formless and undivided."

"Now tell us the characteristics of a true *Yogi*," asked Charpat.

"He is a *Yogi* who washes himself clean
And extinguishes the fire of the body in the Love of God
Who never even in a dream wastes his seed
Such a *Yogi* is no more subject to birth and death
Such a *Yogi* is of the true essence
The supreme essence is formless and undivided."

"What about the *Vairagi* ?" asked Bhartari.

"He is a *Vairagi* who turns back the flow of the life-stream
Fixes his consciousness on the highest
Is engaged in inner meditation night and day
Such a *Vairagi* is of the true essence—
The supreme essence is formless and undivided."

A great crowd gathered round the Guru. He turned to them and said, "We cannot realise truth by observance of outer forms of religion, we can only do so by purifying ourselves and by cultivating virtue. The wearing of ear-rings and the carrying of a begging bowl or smearing the body with ashes does not make one attractive in God's eyes. To please God put on the ear-rings of contentment and replace the begging bowl with begging at His door. Put on the ear-rings of righteousness. Smear thyself with contemplation instead of ashes. Make thy body pure as that of a virgin, before death claims it as its bride. Let the club be the symbol of a disciplined living. By association with the highest, learn the way of gaining victory over the mind. Bow to Him, the first one, of the pure one, the eternal, the immortal, unchanging in all times."

The Guru paused and then spoke again :

"Let others strive for wealth and power ;
Make thy knowledge thy sustenance,
Gather the store of compassion,
Touch the chord of the mind with His name,
Fill the heart with the divine music of the soundless sound.

He is the Lord of all
Union and disunion depend on His will.
His justice metes out the destined share to all
Ignorant men under a wave of emotion
Abandon their own homes and haunt the homes of others.
Having abandoned the duty of a householder
They wander from place to place like castaways.
Without the instruction of the Guru
Their fire of desire is on the increase ;
They fill their bellies like cattle ;
They take ochre and colour their garments,
And put on the disguise of beggars.
They tear up their clothes and make a bag to collect money
They beg from door to door with a blind mind.
They pretend to enlighten the world these men of no honour
Lost in delusion without any sense of honour.
They know not the word
And gamble away their lives.
The unbaked vessel cannot hold the word.
He is a *Sanyasi*, who lost in contemplation of the Guru's word,
Absorbed in it, all his thirst is quenched."

The Sidhas asked him how the fire of desire could be destroyed.

" The fire of desire only the water of the Guru's word can quench," said the Guru. " This fire burns constantly. Devotion does not possess the heart till we serve the Guru ; slandering is a preparation for hell.

" Envy clouds the vision, deluded men wander to places of pilgrimage. The dirt of sin is not thus washed away, it is not thus man can know self.

" They who sift ashes and smear their bodies with it and follow the path of Maya, they know nothing of what is within and without, they recite holy scriptures but indulge in untruth, the true path is not seen by them. They never invoke God or repeat His name and without His grace how can they win peace ? Those whom the Guru does not enlighten cannot see the truth.

" To keep matted hair or shave the head,
They take a vow of silence and become full of conceit
In mad pursuit of wealth, consuming poison instead of nectar
Without overcoming action, without learning to abide by His will.
The mind wandering in all directions without the knowledge of self.
They are no better than animals."

" They whose mind is full of greed," continued the Guru, " who carry a beggar's bowl to beg from door to door
Pretending to instruct.
Ignorant of the truth themselves they are like a cheat of the marketing place,

Full of poison within and show of holiness without
The angel of death shall do its work with them."
" What are the characteristics of a *Sanyasi* ? " asked several voices.
" Listen :
" He is a *Sanyasi* who overcomes the self
And worships God.
Who does not desire a variety of food but is satisfied with that he gets.
Who does not talk but gathers the treasures of forgiveness.
Who banishes darkness with the light of His name
Blessed is the householder, the *Sanyasi*, the *Yogi*,
Who is devoted to the feet of the Lord.
Sanyasi who is without hope or desire
Who brings back his wandering mind under the instruction of the Guru
Who acquires the wealth of the name
Learns to drink the nectar of the Lord
Devoted to one God only
He knows the way.
His mind becomes tranquil and concentrated on reality.
Brahma Vishnu Mahesh are all imbued with the Name
In all the planes, earths, and skies is His light.
When the sound of His name fills the heart
All bliss and all salvation is its reward
Nanak says the truth—
Without His name there is no release from bondage."

75

ONE DAY A REPUTED GYANI CAME TO THE GURU AND discoursed on salvation by knowledge with a great display of learning. The Guru heard him patiently and then asked him, " What do you know of Brahma ? "

" I know all that the Vedas and Shastras teach about him," he answered.

" If salvation can be attained by knowledge, you must surely have attained it."

The Gyani hesitated, he could not honestly say that his knowledge had given him the key to realisation.

The Guru said, " Words are but symbols ; reality itself must be realised to obtain salvation."

" I know all is Brahma," said the Gyani, " but I cannot rid myself of the limitations of my own self."

" This feeling of separation must vanish," said the Guru, " before you can claim knowledge of Him, who is beyond comprehension. All humanity is conscious of its own existence. Only a few can abolish the barriers which I-am-ness raises and become one with him.

" When I am aware of my own self.
Then I am not aware of Him.
When I realise Him,
Then I cease to be.
Now, O Gyani, solve this riddle.
The secret hidden beyond the reach of mind,
The Unknowable dwells in the heart,
He is not discovered without the instruction of the Guru.
It is only when the true teacher is met
We realise that He dwells within.
When self disappears, fear disappears.
And with it the pain of birth and death.

" The pure *budhi* kindled by the Guru realises the Unknowable and cross the ocean of the world.

" Nanak says, repeat Soham Hamsa, I am that, that am I,
And become conscious in all the three states
I am in him but the world is contained in the word.
One cannot become a devotee, said the Guru,
Or gain knowledge without practice of virtue
He who is virtuous becomes the knower,
In virtue knowledge is born.
They who do evil become slaves of evil,
They who do good become embodiments of goodness.
When the measure is full, the duration of life is at an end, the soul is led away ;
When the destined hour arriveth, the soul is led away and all one's relations weep.
The body and soul are separated, O my mother, when one's days are at an end.
Thou hast obtained what was allotted thee and reaped the fruit of thy former acts.
Hail to the Creator, the true King, who allotted to the world its various duties ;
Remember the Lord, O my brethren, all must depart,
The affairs of this world are transitory of short time here.
We must assuredly proceed onward ;
We must assuredly proceed onwards like a gust why should we be proud ?
Repeat the name of Him by whose worship thou shalt obtain happiness in His Court.

In the next world, thou canst in no wise enforce thine authority ; everyone shall fare according to his acts.
Remember the Lord, my brethren, everyone must depart.
That which pleaseth the Omnipotent shall come to pass ; this world is an illusion.
The true Creator pervadeth sea and land, the nether regions and the firmament.
The true Creator is invisible, unequalled ; His limit cannot be found.
Profitable is their advent into this world,
with their whole hearts upon Him.
The adorner by His order demolisheth and again constructeth.
That which pleaseth the Omnipotent shall come to pass. This world is an illusion.
Sayeth Nanak, O father, they weep indeed who weep through love.
If men weep for the sake of wordly things all their weeping,
O fathers, is vain.
All their weeping is in vain, the world is not mindful of God and weepeth for Mammon.
They distinguish not good from evil, and thus lose their human lives.
All who come to this world must depart ; false are they who practise pride.
Sayeth Nanak, men weep indeed, O father, if they weep through love.
For as one thinks, so he becomes
Without virtue life is lived in vain.

" You are right, O Guru," said the Gyani. " How can I purify my *Budhi* which has become dark with the dirt of vice and sin ? "

" Listen," said the Guru :

" Hands, feet and body soiled with dirt
Are washed clean with water.
Clothes which are soiled with dirt
Are washed clean with soap.
A mind that is dirty with misdeeds
Can only be washed clean with the divine Name.
Goodness and badness are not passing terms of speech
Every deed is recorded and the record accompanies us when we depart
What we sow, we shall reap
Nanak says. We come and go
Under the divine law."

" What kind of action should we perform ? " he asked. " And what kind of action should we eschew ? "

" Actions which are performed to gratify the self, actions which harm others, actions which are hypocritical, are evil and should be avoided. Actions which are performed without any personal motive, actions which help others are good. If you are strong, help the weak.

" Remember this body is dwelling place of God ; nothing should be done which is not pleasing to God who is within you. The records of all acts are read out in the presence of the Lord of Justice ; according to their deeds, some draw near and others are driven away even to a greater distance."

" As long as life is in the body, it must perform action. All actions create Karma which governs the present," he said. " Can we sterilise the seed of Karma by any means ? "

" If we surrender ourselves to God and act as the instruments of His will, we sow no seed of action ; the sacrificial fire of devotion consumes the seed of all our actions."

" How can one follow the Divine will ? " asked another. " God gives no direct commands."

" This creation is of God, and when we serve His creation, we serve Him and obey His Commands. When we use our body for the service of others we create no personal Karma, but fulfil the divine purpose, and if every breath of ours is charged with the sacred name, all our acts are then performed in the divine presence."

76

ONE DAY THE GURU WAS SITTING ON THE BANK OF THE river Ravi. A Sikh fell into the river and was almost drowned and lost, when the Guru himself got him out and saved him from being drowned. When the Sikh regained consciousness he fell at the feet of the Guru.

The Guru asked him, " Tell me when you went down the water, what was uppermost in your mind ? "

The Sikh replied, " I had lost all consciousness and desired only one thing—breath."

The Guru addressing all those present said, " When a man becomes unconscious of everything else and desires God with all his power, then he attains *Bhagti*—devotion." The Guru continued, " Taste in the fish, sound in the snake, smell in the bee, passion for light in the moth, and pleasure of touch in the elephant, all of which are desires for the object of the senses, are the causes of their destruction. Brothers, we human beings have not one but five senses to mislead us. In the pursuit of the sense objects we perish. Therefore, have one and one Object alone for all the five senses. Desire only one Object, and that Object will be obtained. Forget yourself entirely in desiring that Object, by desiring which all desires are satisfied.

" Most people profess to love others, but they only love their own selves ; a few love those who love them, but a true devotee of the Guru, a Sikh, must love all, even those who hate him.

" The whole world works for gain, only a few work, because it is their duty to work ; only a rare one works without any desire for a return. But a

Sikh of the Guru must serve friends and foes alike, knowing that it is only thus he can serve God.

Everyone lives for the sake of the self. Some share what they gain with others. A rare one finds enjoyment in giving to others, a true devotee of the Guru, a Sikh, must live entirely for others.

" People endeavour to promote their interest, by aggressiveness. Some people work for personal ends without any aggressiveness. A rare one work for all humanity. A Sikh of the Guru rejoices in carrying out the will of God."

" Most people want their own names to be exalted. A few want their friends to be exalted. There are a few who desire neither name nor fame. A Sikh of the Guru exalts the name of God, without any sense of self."

The Guru about that time seemed to be more and more withdrawing into himself, speaking in parables, and drawing closer to Angad day by day.

77

THE GURU BEGAN TO PREPARE HIMSELF FOR HIS DEPARTURE. He had endowed Angad with his own spirit, but he wanted to prove to his disciples that Angad was worthy to succeed him. He tested him to many ways and proved his faith in himself and his contact with the divine spirit.

Then one day in an open *dewan* he placed Angad on his own seat and bowed to him in acknowledgment. The Guru then left his residence and sat under a withered tree which burst into green foliage.

The news that the Guru had decided to leave the world spread far and wide, and Sikhs flocked round him from all directions. The Guru sat serene and undisturbed and, as usual, spoke to the crowd telling them that his mission had been fulfilled and they would make him happy if they rejoiced with him on his return.

Hail to the Creator, the true King, who allotted to the world its various duties.

When the measure is full, the duration of life is at an end, the soul is led away :

When the destined hour arriveth, the soul is led away and all one's relations weep.

The body and soul are separated, O my mother, when one's days are at an end.

Thou hast obtained what was allotted thee, and reaped the fruit of thy former acts.

Hail to the Creator, the true King, who allotted to the world its various duties ;

Remember the Lord ; O my brethren, all must depart.

The affairs of this world are transitory, a short time here we must assuredly proceed onward ;

We must assuredly proceed onwards like a gust ; why should we be proud ?

Repeat the name of Him by whose worship thou shalt obtain happiness in His Court.

In the next world, thou canst in no wise enforce thine authority; everyone shall fare according to his acts.

Remember the Lord, my brethren everyone must depart.

That which pleaseth the Omnipotent shall come to pass this world is an illusion.

The true Creator pervadeth sea and land, the nether regions and the firmament.

The true Creator is invisible, unequalled; His limit cannot be found.

Profitable is their advent into this world, who have meditated with their whole hearts upon Him.

The adorner by His order demolisheth and again constructeth.

That which pleaseth the Omnipotent shall come to pass, this world is an illusion.

Sayeth Nanak, O father, they shall be considered to have wept who weep through love.

If men weep for the sake of worldly things, all their weeping O father, shall be in vain.

All their weeping shall be in vain, the world is not mindful of God and weepeth for Mammon.

They distinguish not good from evil, and thus lose their human lives.

All who come into this world must depart; false are they who practise pride.

Sayeth Nanak, men shall be considered to have wept, O father, if they weep through love.

The Guru fell into a trance. When he came out of the trance he saw his two sons weeping. He consoled them. Then he asked the Sikhs to sing to *Sohila*. The crowd then sang the *Sohila* and concluded with the last verse of the Japji. Then the Guru drew a white sheet over him. Flowers dropped from the heavens and celestial music was heard.

The Guru passed away on the tenth day of the light half of the month of Asuj in the year Samvat 1595 Vikram (corresponding to 1538 A. D.)

Immediately a dispute arose between the Hindus and Muslims. The former wanted to cremate and the latter wanted to bury him, but when they lifted the sheet, the body of the Guru was not there. So the sheet was cut into two pieces. Half was taken by the Hindus and Sikhs and the other half by the Muslims. A tomb and a *samadh* were erected on the side of the river Ravi. Later these were washed away by the river.